The Hilarion

Connection

Book One

Marlene Swetlishoff

SGP

Symphonies of Grace Publishing

Other books by this author:

The Hilarion Connection©, Book Two

The Hilarion Connection©

Book One

Marlene Swetlishoff

SGP

Symphonies of Grace Publishing

The Hilarion Connection©, Book One

Copyright©2015. Marlene Swetlishoff, for Symphonies of Grace Publishing. www.symphoniesofgrace.com All Rights Reserved.

ISBN: 978-0-9948894-0-9
Marlene Swetlishoff for Symphonies of Grace Publishing
Available from Amazon.com and other retail outlets

Final Proof/Editor - Walter Swetlishoff

Cover Art and Design by Jessica Allain
http://www.enchantedwhispersart.deviantart.com

If you have enjoyed this book, your honest review on Amazon.com would be greatly appreciated!

For the Glory of God
In whose Infinite light, love, grace and goodness
We all live, move and have our being.

Acknowledgements

Thank you to Isabelle E. Baillie, Geomancer/Master Dowser, Channeler, Prolific Mystic Poet, and Keeper of the Mysteries of Creation, for your friendship and for helping me to believe in my ability to bring forward the truths, guidance and inspiration from the spiritual dimensions, the Angelic realms and the Ascended Master realms. For one year as I began to receive messages, you steadfastly checked each message I received in order to ensure their high light and truth content. You, my friend, are a pearl beyond price!

Thank you to Vello Reili, for the belief that I had it in me to write books that can create positive change in the world. You are another blessing in my life! Your support made this publication a reality. I thank you from the bottom of my heart!

Thank you to the following beautiful people who voluntarily and faithfully translated the messages within the time frame contained in this book for www.therainbowscribe.com

Esther Abreu, Canada – Spanish
Helena Renner, Brazil – Portuguese
Mara Brante, Latvia - Latvian
Dr. Stephan Kaula, Germany – German

What People are Saying:

As I read and re-read The Hilarion Connection©, Book One, the message that it conveys became clear to me. It is simply the fact that humanity must and will evolve in their spiritual process until their love for each and every human being is manifest on Earth. The Divine conception of life is the inevitable and final spiritual evolution which could be expressed simply as Heaven on Earth. Until his death in 1910, Leo Tolstoy was perhaps one of the best known personalities in the world. People from all continents – ordinary readers, politicians, writers, and philosophers went on pilgrimages to his estate in Russia, hoping to learn and understand about the changes that were coming in the future for humanity.

Leo Tolstoy in his book entitled "The Kingdom of God is Within You" exemplifies the doctrine of love for humanity. In it, Tolstoy wrote that to achieve the Divine social conception of life, one must go within where love is the essence of the soul and thinking is the essence of the heart. We must believe and understand that each and every human being has God within them.

The desire within every human heart longs for a lasting love between humanity and yet our external expression of love does not exceed beyond the love of nation we were born into, apart from love for self, family and community. The transference from love of self to family and relatives is accomplished easily and naturally but the transference to love of community and nation is more difficult and requires special training. To love all humanity can only be achieved if each and every human recognizes the Creator within them and trains their thinking to come from the heart. The achievement of this concept is clearly explained in Marlene's book.

Walter Swetlishoff, Tech/Eng., B.Ed., M.Ed., B.C. Canada

~*~*~*~

It was in 2005 that I first learned about the Ascension from a wonderful healer Betty who became one of my best friends in the last several years. I was guided to read the Rainbow Scribe website and since then I have religiously read it every week, sometimes twice a week. Since it is easier for me to read the information from a printed copy, I have collected innumerable pages from the Rainbow Scribe.

As a healer, physician and visionary, I was drawn to the messages from Master Hilarion. In the beginning it was as if I needed to know what he said before making any decisions for the week. Then I advanced to the next level and I needed clarity about various aspects of my life. Each week Master Hilarion replied with such synchronicity. It feels as if I have been attending his university of Higher Learning and now I have ascended to a higher level whereby I AM trusting my own Intuitive guidance and gifts more. His messages are a confirmation of what I already know in my Heart.

From my Heart Palace, I AM truly "Greatful" for these literary gifts of Magic. Thank you, Marlene for Being His Voice. With love, light, JOY and Beauty,
Berta Maria Hines, M.D., U.S.A.

~*~*~*~

I would like to thank you for your outstanding efforts for the Rainbow Scribe website. Master Hilarion's weekly messages are absolutely amazing and inspirational.

I first became aware of Master Hilarion's book The Nature of Reality in 2011 under the most remarkable circumstances and my life has been in a continuous transformational growth/expansion process ever since. Some the information within Master Hilarion's weekly messages seems uncannily close to home. On many occasions, it feels a little as though the messages are directed to me personally.

There is much information in this world and from many sources. Master Hilarion's information has empowered me to put many parts of life's puzzle together in such a way as to embark on a project (thus far in theory) where upon numerous energetic modalities can be brought together to tap into, greatly amplify, retransmit and direct into where they may be required. For example: Assisting in the healing of the Animal Kingdom, Humanity's relationship to the Animal Kingdom and the Healing and Ascendency process of the Earth. Thank you so much for your very important and inspirational work.

D.M., Adelaide, South Australia

~*~*~*~

I was fortunately led to discover this website in 2010. It started as a growing love for Rainbows to the extent that I could spend some time googling on it. I found a lot of information including this site. Since then, I am enjoying the opportunity of reading it whenever I want. It has seen me gaining spiritual heights and I am really thankful to both the Ascending Beings and the Hosts of Heaven responsible.

S. Muchemwa,Zimbabwe

~*~*~*~

Hilarion has been a part of my Sunday rituals for years now. I believe I began reading the channelings sometime after 10-10-10, and I always look forward to the messages as they offer insight and quite often validation for the thoughts, feelings and energies that I experience during the week. (I love that!) Hilarion reminds me daily to walk in nature, drink plenty of fresh water and breath well to assist in circulation of the energies. This message is so ingrained that I find myself thanking him for the reminder; consequently, he has become a part of my daily life, and truly a beautiful guide that offers discipline as a tool to shift energies and pivot when needed. I AM grateful for the help, and really grateful for the constant connection to this brilliant and helpful Ascended Master.

I AM, Hilary! Sacramento, California.

~*~*~*~

Table of Contents

Foreword

Last year, I found a request in my INBOX – on a spiritual website that both Marlene and I are on—"asking for a favor" and that was to write a "Foreword" to this compilation of Hilarion's Weekly Messages.

I couldn't have been more surprised – all the more that I had only "connected" to Hilarion's sharings – via Marlene – since June 2012.

But to my utter astonishment, I uttered a YES with a fervent spontaneity that I have never known in my life! With a cautious, discriminating and discerning VIRGO on the Ascendant in my natal holographic Zodiac this was totally "out of character."

I proceeded to download and print all of Hilarion's Weekly Messages since the beginning of the year, and in true Virgo fashion, even researched WHO Hilarion was in former lifetimes. Simply had to get a "flavoring" of this Magical Guy that held me in such a pleasant spell and who was terribly helpful – in a practical, down-to-earth manner—in navigating the new, incoming energies.

And woo-hoo – in his last incarnation, discovered that Hilarion was St. Hilarion – an ascetic monk in Palestine who had amazing healing gifts. In addition, he had had an incarnation as PLATO so, was simply thrilled and thought, "OK, I can work with this!" As I read the incredibly nurturing and nourishing Messages, I became truly hooked to this incredible energy stream of such LOVE, WISDOM and HEALING. Fantastic. This was working for me. But then I considered the "vessel" or "vehicle" through which these timely messages, via Hilarion, were coming through. There was an uncanny familiarity with the energy called Marlene Swetlishoff...a very comforting and reassuring energy. And "voila" – it resembled a maternal grandmother who was Mother Earth personified!

I love words...but what I love more is the ENERGY behind the words. Although Marlene resonates as a pure conduit and scribe, she has an energy signature that resonates intricately with Hilarion and his emphasis of "bringing Heaven to Earth." This is not spirituality that is in "escapist mode"—ie. "get me out of here as quickly as possible" – but the DEEPEST LOVE possible for Mother Earth, which for me, epitomizes Marlene's energy. And that energy reverberates in every filament of my being!

The compilation of these Messages is truly a GIFT in the full sense of the word: an unconditional giving of Marlene's personhood – her time and energy—in conjunction with that of Master Hilarion—whose healing gifts are legendary.

HEALING, in the full sense of the word, means "coming into whole-ness" – body/mind/spirit. Not one element is less than another – merely a difference in energetic modality.

As I continued to read the Messages – mostly backtracking to the beginning of the year – it felt like a "homecoming" – coming back to Source, to All That Is ... to UNITY CONSCIOUSNESS or Unity in Diversity.

The Messages were expressed with elegance and simplicity; the sentences flowed effortlessly and with ease; the depth and wisdom were sheer MAGIC with the recurrent theme advising to be grounded and centered as we anchor in the higher energies streaming in full force from the higher realms.

Marlene, like a Mother Earth Shaman, is not only a clear conduit and scribe, but the quintessential cheerleader, counselor, facilitator and Loving Nurturer for those going through the "bumps" and "ruts" on the Path. She is patient and understanding – COMPASSIONATE – beyond measure.

There are "channels" and there are "channels." When the message is tinged with unadulterated LOVE and fathomless WISDOM – expressed with clarity and elegant simplicity – I think something very special touches – and forever changes our spirit and soul. Marlene is the loving, magical, spiritual ALCHEMIST – via the loving grace of Hilarion - in helping us move forward on our spiritual/consciousness journeys.

I couldn't be more grateful and appreciative – these Messages nourish and nurture my motivation to proceed onwards – they are loving and catalytic. What more can one ask?

In LOVE, LIGHT JOY…and GRATITUDE to Hilarion and Marlene.

~*~*~*Eva Sophia~*~*~*

Eva Sophia is a certified Life Coach living in Santa Fe, New Mexico, U.S.A. under her professional name Hilkka Constantin. She can be reached at: h.constantin@comcast.net

Preface

In a message to Marlene, the Scribe, through the incomparable trance channel Edwin Courtenay from the United Kingdom in July 2014, Hilarion said this to her:

"Ours is a joyous union, a happy connection, a positive link. We are not aligned, you and I because of karma, because of imbalance, because of disharmony, but rather we are aligned through love, positivity and hope - hope that combined, our Light might bring opening and awakening for others, in healing and truth, positivity, restoration, resolution and peace.

Now is indeed the time for us to move forwards, to stride out into the world together, aligned, connected as One. Now the path opens up before you, and you the herald, the messenger, you the student of the Master, the disciple of the Wise, carries forth the rod of power, the rod of Asclepius, that you may bless all those that you may encounter on your way, not only with healing but also with teaching and understanding, that these individuals might know what is to be done, what they might do to heal themselves and transform their own personal healing journey as they walk upon their way.

I, Hilarion, am Ascended Master, Patron of Healers, Custodian of the wisdom and the secrets of ancient Atlantis, Awakener of Truth regarding the ancient healing powers and how they might be now applied in this contemporary world and you are one of my heralds and together our Light shall shine, spread out upon the world connecting with those others who work for me in similar ways, that we might form a conglomerate, a league, a cooperative of Truth, sharing understanding, and disseminating peace.

You asked about yourself as my scribe. Of course, you are much more than this. You are my teacher, my doctor; you are my priest, my priestess, my nurse. Your work is not simply to convey the essence of my understanding through the power of the written but also to tend to the people's needs directly, through healing and the transmission of Light and to guide other people in how they might use this Light to heal themselves and others, applying the principles of healing to every aspect of their life. There is an important aspect of your work which is connected to my words and voice, to becoming my scribe and translator in order that my Truth might find expression in your world.

As you have accurately already deduced, it is a book, a series of written words that I desire to bring forwards through you. It is my hope, my desire, that this communicated material will become a book that will be published and distributed out into the world. "

This book was written over many years and is a compilation of the hugely popular discourses that the Ascended Master Hilarion brings through this Scribe. These messages are sought by thousands of people throughout the world and continue to be published on: www.therainbowscribe.com

Introduction

The Ascended Master Hilarion is the Atlantian Ascended Master who holds the knowledge, the wisdom and the power of Atlantis for the Ascended Master Collective, for although many other Ascended Masters experienced Atlantis and lived and served in its Temples, Hilarion was the one who has had the most incarnations there. It is during these times that I made 'the Hilarion connection' and was told by Hilarion recently that in nearly every lifetime that he had known in Atlantis, I was there also, sometimes in great and powerful ways and other times, our connection was fleeting and minimal.

His most famous lifetime in Atlantis was as Hilarion, the High Priest in the Temple of Peace, which was the Topaz Temple, the Temple of Healing. He was the coordinator and facilitator for training those who were chosen to become Healers in Atlantis. He was responsible for diversifying the training into many different areas.

He discovered that hidden amongst the different caste systems, were healing modalities, understandings and truths that were powerful and essential and he brought these back to the Temple of Peace in Atlantis.

He brought experts, Elders, High Priests and High Priestesses from these castes and made them teachers in the Temple of Peace. It was unheard of - for no one before him had ever done such a thing. No High Priest or High Priestess had ever considered that there might be value in the healing systems of other castes.

He pioneered this outreach and connection and sent Priests and Priestesses out into the world to not only share their truths and knowledge but to learn from those that they encountered. Many returned with knowledge that enriched Atlantis and they also passed on guidance and teachings from the Temple of Peace that enriched the world.

Hilarion has incarnated in many ensuing lifetimes since the five epochs of Atlantis. Throughout his many lifetimes, he remained committed to bringing forth Divine Truth to help humanity remember their magnificent origin and facilitate their healing.

He comes again in this current time to our contemporary world which is evolving, transforming and shifting, through his chosen channels/scribes to help the Earth and humanity ascend into a higher Light and consciousness, which is their true state of being. This process of awakening and remembrance is called Ascension. He overlights and guides the souls of humanity from his retreat at the Temple of Truth in the etheric realms above the island of Crete through his many chosen channels and scribes. The words in this book are through one of his scribes.

What is Ascension? The Mayan timekeepers indicated that 2012 marked the close of several large cycles of time: a 26,000 year Mayan Calendar cycle, a 78,000 year Earth cycle, a 26 million year Earth cycle and a 225 million Galactic Year. The simultaneous close of these cycles in December 2012 was a moment when humanity, Planet Earth, and all of Creation took a simultaneous leap in evolution. This very rare cosmic event has been exposing our whole solar system to intense cycles of cosmic energy.

This energy source emanating from Galactic Center is activating our DNA and has set into motion a shift in the Earth and in the physical bodies of humanity to a higher level of vibration and frequency. Many people are currently finding the transformation into a higher state of consciousness a difficult process.

Hilarion and all of the Ascended Masters of the Family of Light are working steadfastly with all who are awake and aware and the countless others who are in the process of awakening to the immense opportunity for quantum growth on their evolutionary soul journey that now lies before them. The following chapters are the words that Hilarion brings to all those who choose to be a conscious part of the new Earth reality, a world of peace, and higher consciousness. These words continue to uplift, inspire and empower people across the world to focus their attention and intention on the manifestation of an incredible Golden Age of enlightened, peaceful, and illumined living.

Thank you, Dear Reader, for making the Hilarion connection! May you be blessed beyond measure because of it!

- Chapter 1 -
The Transmissions Begin

These messages to you, Dear Ones, are brought with great love from the higher dimensions of Light. I am very happy to be able to come to you in this way, for we of the Family of Light have much to impart to those who have the ears to hear and the eyes to see.

Many people on the planet Earth are beginning to or will soon be awakening. This requires, for those who have already been awakened, greater understanding, empathy and compassion, for sometimes the awakenings will bring up much that has been hidden beneath the surface of each person. If you see tendencies in those around you that include:

1. Unreasonable anger
2. Impatience
3. Depression
4. Confusion
5. Questioning
6. Fear
7. Projections
8. Great tiredness
9. Low energy
10. Weeping

Remember, Dear Ones, this is the path that you have already walked. It is important not to match the energy; rather, radiate peace, calm and loving kindness. Great patience is required and the utmost of respect towards your sister or brother.

One must stay detached so as not to enter into the emotions that are being expressed at every moment. This is why we have been working with you beyond sleep, to help you clear all that no longer serves you on your path in order to assist your loved ones and those you have frequent contact with.

This is now the time of the living Masters walking upon the Earth. Many more of you are waking up to your destiny and mission, and the remembrance of why you have come. Walk your path with integrity and impeccability.

I wish to address those who are called Lightworkers, those who have consistently and persistently throughout the years, given of their life energies to hold and bring in the Light. There has been much good that has been created and there is more still to be manifested and brought into being. I want to let you know that we of your Family of Light from the highest dimensions are very pleased with what has been accomplished. We have moved the Earth and all upon her into the fifth dimensional frequencies. All that remains is for humankind to 'catch up', so to speak, and this is our next step in the Divine Plan.

The higher cosmic energies have been pouring onto the Earth and are lifting and awakening you and those around you into a greater realization of your Divine origins, and this activity will continue to record levels. Because of this, there will be a greater need for knowledge to be available to these awakened ones where they can come to learn how they may be of greater service to the Light, how they may help themselves raise their frequency levels, and indeed, what the Divine Plan is all about.

What does it mean to raise your frequency level? Anytime anyone reaches up to God Source and speaks from their heart through prayers, decrees or invocations, it immediately raises their vibration and frequency level to a higher octave, and by doing so, it also increases the frequency level and octave of your planet. Think of the possibilities, if in unison, humankind joined together as One Voice, One Thought, at One global time; the miracles that would be created upon this Earth could only be termed as 'miraculous'.

However, we are dealing with the now. Right at the moment, there are many people who are awakening and they are going through the process of dealing with releasing all that was not dealt with within themselves through their entire lifetime and in many cases, former lifetimes. This process will continue to increase and accelerate as one Galactic cycle of approximately 26,500 years has come to an end and a new one has begun.

The cosmic energies that are coming onto your planet are of unconditional love from the higher dimensions of God's kingdoms and that is why it brings up everything that is not in resonance with it. We, your Family of Light, wish all who have already awakened and are 'seasoned Lightworkers', to bear within you great patience, compassion and love, to radiate peace and calm to these individuals who are awakening, for you are now the beacons of Light that they shall turn to and you have a great and solemn responsibility to hold your Light with impeccability, integrity and constancy.

Always work through your heart center. Follow your inner promptings and in any instance, ask for assistance and clarification if needed. You are surrounded by many, many Beings of Light, Angels of Light, who are just waiting to assist you. This is a Divine dispensation that has come from Prime Creator. You are now being assisted to become of assistance to others, and although it may seem a little strange to you compared to your former life duties and daily activities that you have been used to, this is something that you will need to adapt to and integrate into your daily activities, for as everything else in life, it is just a new way to get used to.

There are many upon this planet who wish to impede your progress, who wish to impede the awakening of the masses of humanity and these beings work in subtle ways but those who are of the Light can immediately sense within themselves when the energy is not of the highest vibration and can immediately clear themselves of these energies of the lower vibrations.

In the coming years, things shall change dramatically for the betterment of the Earth and everyone upon her. These are the times,

Dear Ones, when the Light returns to Earth. Continue to radiate and stand in your Light, to integrate the higher frequencies as they come in so that you can help your sisters and brothers around you. I come with the blessings from all of the Family of Light whom I am representing.

I would like to speak to you now about decreeing and what it actually means when you decree. We of the Family of Light daily participate in decreeing. That is how important decrees are, Dear Ones! When you sit and focus all your attention on the words, purpose and intention of a decree and you state it verbally, you are in fact, asserting your authentic sovereignty of the divine essence of your being. You are by the very fact that you are stating the decree, proclaiming your power as a co-creator with God. When you decree a thing, it makes it so, if done consistently!

You have a great and solemn responsibility to hold your Light with impeccability, integrity and constancy.

If the majority of you decreed each day, the world would change quickly into that which we all desire, which is Heaven on Earth, an Earth ascended into the fifth dimension and restored to her original pristine beauty. It is important for you to realize that when you do this, you not only add power and energy to the Light for the purpose of creating greater goodness in the world, you also add power to your own Light. It is cumulative. Please bear this in mind when we ask you to decree a thing in unison with the Family of Light, for that is what is involved.

Beloved Ones, what does it mean to be a Lightworker? A Lightworker has an awareness of the Flame of God that never dies and it is this Flame that burns brightly within your hearts as you seek to anchor the Light of the Divine on Earth so that this Flame, this spark of the Divine re-ignites within every human heart.

No matter what happens in your outer circumstances, you always have this Flame of God within you that you instinctively turn to and you fan that Flame to burn ever brighter. When you read or see a request for assistance in a worldwide focus, you as a Lightworker, participate and contribute your energies. You see the inherent value of saying decrees each day, you see the value of prayers and affirmations, you see the value of worldwide meditations and focuses and you give of your energy and time to add Light to the world in these ways. No matter what else happens, it is your greatest focus and passion to add more Light and positive energy to the world. That is what a Lightworker is, and does. Even though you may feel that what you are doing does not help that much, you still do it and by doing so, you add great Light to the world.

> **Even though you may feel that what you are doing does not help that much, you still do it and by doing so, you add great Light to the world.**

Beloved Ones, in this momentous time in the world's history, it is so important to keep on focusing on the Light, the Light that you are, the Flame of God within your heart, fanning it, spreading it, radiating it out into the world. That is how important you are!

The days ahead of us are filled with momentous revelations; people will be awakening quickly and will be questioning the so called "authorities" which they never even thought to question before. People will be awakening in masses upon every corner of the world. There will come forth people power, there will come forth the Light of truth, there will come forth the demand from people worldwide for integrity in their leaders, for accountability in their leaders, and not just in their governments, but in all the old institutions that have governed this world for eons of time. And it is the people themselves who will bring positive changes, simply by the fact of their increasing numbers, as they share the same thought, which is to create positive change into Truth, into Integrity, into Light, into Love, into Peace. This will manifest, Dear Ones!

In the coming days, keep focusing on the Light. Keep decreeing 'The Great Invocation'. This simple invocation is more powerful than you can imagine. We, your Family of Light in the Ascended Light realms, decree this even now! It is a part of what you could call our 'daily' practice. When you join with us on a daily basis (noontime/midnight) with this decree, miracles are being created! Your assistance is invaluable in all that you do. Let us keep on working together!

I would like to speak to you about working on yourselves. Now what does that mean, working on yourselves? It means becoming attuned to the greater Light and higher spiritual precepts. It means setting a goal, for example, of raising your frequency level and then finding the means and ways to do this. Then practicing this each and every day consistently to accomplish the raising of your frequency, which is what is necessary if you want to increase it. We have talked about decreeing as a method to do this. This is an excellent way to increase your vibration and frequency. Prayer is another method; even asking for your frequency level to be increased incrementally each day of your Divine self will accomplish this.

Another way of working on yourself is observing your daily habits. How do you spend your day? Do you have a balance in your life? Do you work *and* play? Do you take time to eat properly? Do you go for a walk in the fresh air and connect with nature? This is very necessary for you to do in order to ground yourself into the crystalline core of Mother Earth so that you are attuned to her energy. It also helps your body maintain its health and vitality.

Another method of working on yourself is to practice daily deep breathing exercises. This is an excellent method of purifying your body, your mind, and your thoughts, and for increasing the frequency of each of your chakras in your entire body system. Deep breathing accomplishes this by bringing in pranic energy through the breath. It is the energy of life giving substance and also contains electrical and magnetic particles. It is a really good idea to breath deeply and by breathing deeply, I mean not into your chest but down into your sacral and root chakras, as far down as you could get the breath, holding it there as long as it is comfortable and then when expelling that breath, visualizing and intending that all impurities be moved out of your bodily system through your outgoing breath.

I shall now give you a deep breathing exercise that will greatly accelerate your frequency level and purification process. For this exercise you need to be standing with your feet firmly planted about a foot apart, then expel all of your breath as much as possible down to your root chakra, then breathe in and as you are breathing in, picture pranic energy in the form of White Light coming down, all the way down to your root chakra where it circles in a loop and on your outgoing breath, it picks up all the impurities and as you expel your breath, you are eliminating those impurities from your body, physically, mentally, emotionally and spiritually. The intent to do this helps immensely to make it more effective.

It is your thoughts that create your reality.

If you have been a shallow breather all your life, this will be a difficult procedure for you to adapt to but if you persist you will find it extremely helpful, as one of the benefits to this exercise is that all of your chakras are cleansed, charged and revitalized with life giving energy. There should be a repetition of these breaths in one session that should be seven breaths with no great pauses in between the in breath and the out breath. For those of you who are shallow breathers, this might not be possible at first without a feeling of dizziness, but if you gradually persist, it will improve.

Working on yourselves also means watching your thought processes. Now this is crucial, Dear Ones, for it is your thoughts that create your reality. When one is on the spiritual path, one learns to be in control of one's thoughts. If you have a running commentary in your mind, criticizing yourself, not liking how you look, how your hair looks, how your eyes look, how your face looks, how your body looks, and you are mentally beating yourself up in your mind; that is what will manifest in your physical reality which will be mirrored to you through the experiences that come to you! It is very important that you realize this and start to create thoughts of what you want rather than on what you don't want. Be patient with yourselves. This is where daily decreeing or doing affirmations comes in as a very powerful means for those who are not used to disciplining themselves in this way. Decreeing or affirming positive and powerful statements several times each day keeps you focused on the good you wish to create.

You'll notice your life starting to change wonderfully, becoming more positive in every way!

Find those decrees or those affirmations that state clearly what you want and that it must always be for the highest good for all concerned. That phrase must be always added at the end of your decree or affirmation; and then begin to say this each day. That too, is working on yourself and creating a positive reality in your daily existence. As you keep doing this, you will notice yourself becoming more proficient in this practice. You'll notice your life starting to change wonderfully, becoming more positive in every way, for as you give your energetic intention into the world through this practice, you in turn receive. You are the creator, Dear Ones; that is how powerful you are! Keep that in mind, your thoughts are powerful, as are you, more powerful than you have been able to conceive so far.

Another aspect of working on yourselves involves working with your ego. There is a balance to be achieved, you cannot kill the ego, the ego is necessary in order to exist and survive in the reality in which you are now manifesting. The challenge here is to recognize that the ego could be used to help you progress on your spiritual path. You must also recognize that you need to be balanced, with a healthy self esteem and self respect but without arrogance and a sense of superiority over others. That is not working for your own highest good or anyone else's. That just delays your progress in increasing your vibration and frequency, and that is what Ascension is all about, Dear Ones, increasing your vibration and frequency. These are some methods and ideas for you to think on and practice.

There is also the need to follow through on your intentions. In this day and age, we realize that you are extremely busy in your lives. The world system that has been created and perpetuated keeps you ever with your nose to the grindstone, having to do this and having to do that. There are many 'should's' in your lives and it is very hard from one day to the next to keep a focus on the good that you intend to create for yourselves.

It is very important and crucial that you take the time to establish a routine that you follow through on each and every day. Set your intentions in writing, create a format that you use each day and it will become as though it is second nature to you, Dear Ones. This is how to establish a new beginning, a new change or routine in your life for that which you wish to create in your life.

Alchemy is created by steadfastly and persistently working your plan, your intention, for the good you wish to create in your world.

Even though you may have distractions, you have your daily format set before you and as you keep on working your plan, it becomes easier and before you know it, you are falling into the creation of what you intend! This is a very important concept that must be grasped by you. This is what we, the Ascended Masters, talk about when we say 'alchemy' and 'magic'; alchemy is created by steadfastly and persistently working your plan, your intention, for the good you wish to create in your world and within your own selves, I might add.

The first step is to take the time to focus and clarify what it is that you intend, what it is that you wish to create in your life or within yourself and then write this out, so that you have it on your desk where you could see it first thing in the morning. Start each day affirming or decreeing this out loud to your self and out into the airwaves, for this is how the Universe answers you. It is a basic law of the Universe that you must 'Ask and ye shall receive'. You must *ask*!

Setting forth your plan, your intention, of what you wish to create and then following through each day will bring to you what you wish to create. It is simply that simple, Dear Ones! Realize how powerful you truly are. Each of you is a creator! It is very important at this time to realize this and begin to train your minds in the way that you wish your life to go. It is your thoughts that create what you desire in your life, or conversely, create what you do not desire, if that is where your thoughts dwell. That is why it is vital to start training and disciplining yourselves and this is a very simple but very effective method of doing so. For we of the Family of Light, it is very heartening to see and take note that there are more of you who are realizing your own power, taking our counsel and implementing your plan and working your plan.

It is a basic law of the Universe that you must ask!

Dear Ones, you are creating magic, wonderful magic, the magic of being in your own power, the magic of creating your own reality! You have always been doing this but you have not been consciously aware of this creating. It was hard for you to see the connection between your intentions, whether conscious or unconscious, because it took time for that which you intended or that which was unintentionally created, to come forth as manifested experience in your reality. It took time for that to happen and one really had to be very aware in order to realize this. Now, in these new times, in these new energies, that which you want to create in your life is becoming much easier and comes much faster to you.

This is a double edged sword. You must also ensure that your thoughts are always highly beneficial for yourself and others, always in alignment for the greatest good of all concerned. This practice requires self discipline and this is how you come into your own mastery and become the Masters walking the Earth. It is all about discipline, Dear Ones.

There are so many of you upon the Earth now who are awake and who wish to be of greater service to the Light. We ask you to set this intention in your plan and ask each day. Your spiritual Guides, your spiritual higher dimensional Teachers and others who are in the higher realms will take note of your intention and what it is that you desire, they will look at your overall plan and they will assist you in heading into the direction that you wish to go. We are here to assist each of you to gain your Mastership, to remember the Masters that you truly are. We do require your request though, Dear Ones, for you live on a free will planet. What that means is you must ask for what you want; you must ask the Universe for what you want. It will not come to you otherwise. So make your plan and work your plan.

We are here to assist each of you to gain your Mastership, to remember the Masters of Self that you truly are.

We are very excited to have so many of you reach out and ask us for that which is your heart's desire. We are so pleased to be working with you to accomplish your spiritual goals and at the same time, the working of the Divine Plan which creates that Heaven on Earth that we all desire to bring into manifestation on the Earth. If you could see the legions of Angels and the thousands of Ascended Masters and Lady Masters who are just waiting for you to *ask* for their assistance so that they can leap into action to help you in every possible way, you would be astounded! There are many Masters and Lady Masters (the Family of Light) that you are not aware of, Dear Ones, but they stand ready to serve you and work with you. So do call upon us. We are here to work in unison with you to accomplish your spiritual life goals to step into your own Mastery.

Let us continue our discourse on the art, science and alchemy of decreeing. Many of you are wondering why there is this continuous ongoing message from the Family of Light who mention in almost every message the word, 'decreeing', encouraging you to decree. This is a way to stand in your power as I have mentioned previously. This is a way to rise up into your Divine selves, a way to connect with your Divine selves, that God spark within you.

When you decree, you are standing up and saying to the spiritual world that you are a Master manifesting upon the Earth plane. When you say your decree and repeat the words that call upon the spiritual forces and all the Beings of Light and you do this each day, you give permission to all the great Light Beings on the highest dimensions of Light, on the highest planes of existence, to come and amplify your intentions.

There is not too much that can be accomplished unless you remember your Mastership and call upon us so that we have permission to come into your Earth reality and help make the great changes that you are decreeing. We can do this, Dear Ones, when you ask, and that is how we are working together in unity. It is so exciting for the Family of Light to have this connection and partnership with each of you. So much good is being accomplished as you ask when you are decreeing that it all be for the highest good of all concerned.

When we look upon the Beacons of Light that you are becoming, the Light that you are generating and we see these Beacons lighting up all over the world, it just gladdens our hearts. On all levels of the Family of Light - the Planetary Council, the Galactic Council, and the Cosmic Council, we stand in awe and appreciation. We are so grateful for this connection and partnership.

There is also the need to remember to ground yourselves. Please remember to do this. As you do your decreeing, and you complete your decrees, ground the energies into the center of Mother Earth as your final step. In this way, you are bringing the higher Light into the Earth plane and anchoring it within the crystalline core of Mother Earth. You have no idea how beneficial this is. The more Light that is anchored into the crystalline core of Mother Earth, the more Light filters through onto every facet of life on Earth and enters the field of consciousness of the masses, the more their minds turn to that which is good, that which is sacred, that which is precious.

As you can tell, there is a great division taking place at this time. There are those who have not yet awakened who see only that which is wrong with the world. Then there are those such as you who see all that the others see, but bravely and courageously intend, affirm and decree that which they *want* in this world. You are such powerful beings, Dear Ones! When you stand in your Light and you decree what you want, you are being magicians and alchemists, bringing forth the new Earth reality, the world that we all want to see manifesting as the Great Golden Age. This is happening and it is being done with your free will offerings in your partnership with us, your Spiritual, Planetary, Galactic and Cosmic Councils, your Family of Light.

Lightworkers are asked to unite in their efforts. They are asked to stand in their Light, to decree for that which they have been working towards for such a long time, always with the caveat that it be for the highest good for all. This is a very crucial time and that is why we keep coming and asking you to issue your decrees each day. It is helping to anchor the Light firmly and deeply within the Earth. Mother Earth's gratitude knows no bounds. I know that many of you have felt her gratitude as you are decreeing because it has brought you to tears when you felt it. It is also gratitude from the higher planes; the Spiritual, Planetary, Cosmic Family of Light, for the great good that is being accomplished could not be so quickly manifested without your daily efforts.

Know that we always stand by your side and are always with you no matter what transpires in your daily lives; remember that you never walk alone. We, your Teachers and Guides, your friends and spiritual comrades, walk always by your side.

- Chapter 2 -
A Glimpse Into The Future

The days that are coming will be filled with much that holds shocking energies and this is why we ask you, the Lightworkers, to ground Light into the Earth and to hold your Light, to believe in yourselves and to be the Light because the Light is what will create the balance that is necessary in the days ahead.

We have been working with all of you beyond sleep. You have all been in training. You are our 'front line' and you are all so very necessary for the Divine Plan to move ahead. Know, Dear Ones, that you are blessed in all ways, that you are protected, that each of your beloved family members are protected as well, for we understand that you need to be free of all worries in order to fully focus on your mission of grounding the Cosmic Light into the Earth at this time. Know that you and your loved ones are under our full protection.

We, your Family of Light, hold forth at this most auspicious time the Cosmic Christ love, energy and power and we are directing it to pour upon the Earth. As this occurs, it opens up new waves of consciousness in the minds of humanity. It opens up waves of awakening that hasn't happened in millennia and as this process continues, people will start speaking up and questioning all that is happening around them which they never questioned before. This will create rapid and great change upon this planet. Humanity has begun to understand with the help of these great cosmic energies that are pouring in, that they have the power; that they need to take action; that they need to speak up. They are realizing that they can do this in a peaceful manner by standing in their their truth and not being willing to accept anything other than that.

Humanity has begun to understand that they have the power; that they need to take action; that they need to speak up.

The days ahead are filled with exciting probabilities and possibilities and it is all a matter of free will choice for the people of Earth. All that needs to be brought into the Light shall be brought into the Light of awareness. All that needs to be examined and released will be brought to the surface. Because of you, Beloved Lightworkers, this will happen without too much chaos. This will happen peacefully and naturally and the way will, miraculously, open up for humanity to step into the Golden Age.

All is well, Dear Ones. Those who have longed for peace shall see it taking root upon this Earth. Those who have longed for a world of joy, harmony and purity shall see this taking root in the consciousness of humanity. All that no longer vibrates to the goodness that is our Creator will be released and will melt away. All that is not of the Light of our Creator will be released. We stand at your side to magnify your energies, to assist you in every way, for you are the Light Emissaries upon this Earth. It is through you that the great changes are taking place.

Know that the Great Being, Gaia/ Mother Earth is ever so grateful for all of your assistance and that in the days ahead you will be blessed beyond measure, for as you bless all those upon the Earth with your energies in this way, so are you blessed. Keep shining your beautiful light upon this Earth for your combined Light is merging into rainbow Light all over the Earth and it is a beautiful sight to behold.

The crystalline frequencies of the new Earth reality are daily filling your energy bodies, are daily purifying and bringing into greater power, your light body. What a wonderful sight to behold! We, from our perspective, are absolutely delighted to see your beautiful energies light up this world.

Remain true to your essential selves, your Divine selves, focus only upon that which is good, that which is right, that which is of your highest integrity and intention for your new Earth reality and continue, Dear Ones. This is a golden opportunity and you are holding the Light for the rest of humanity at this time in order to pave the way for them to see the opportunities open before them to enter into the new Earth reality. This is what is occurring at this time.

I, Hilarion, on behalf of your Family of Light call upon Lightworkers everywhere in this world to unite and stand in your Light, for you are the hope of the world. Let nothing stop you from remembering this. I ask you to focus upon grounding the energies into the Earth and to just continue decreeing, to continue visualizing your best and highest good for yourselves, your beloved family members, for humanity and Mother Earth. Know that you are performing a most needed and vital service.

You are holding the Light for the rest of humanity at this time.

The Earth is transitioning through the fourth dimension (a higher octave) and that means that you are too. This is an interim dimension; this is why at this time you are being cleansed along with the Earth, of all that does not vibrate with the fifth dimension octave and frequency where the Earth is heading. That is why there is such a great cleansing happening. Within you, anything that is coming up for your awareness is not in resonation with the fifth dimension consciousness which is Earth's destination and the destination of all of you, so be patient with yourselves, Dear Ones, for this is an ongoing, necessary and in the long run, very beneficial happening.

It is cleansing all emotions, all hidden thoughts, all that needs to be observed, looked at and released so that you can move on. It is also happening in the Earth Mother. There is much that is occurring, being released and transmuted at this time. There are many upon the higher dimensions who work to assist in this capacity, and are helping to ease the Earth and humanity into the fifth dimension of consciousness with safety, grace, and ease.

The crystalline frequencies of the new Earth reality are daily filling your energy bodies, are daily purifying and bringing into greater power, your light body.

Dear Ones, there are not many different Earths, there is this one dear Earth and she is changing and transforming and so are you. Now while you are traversing the fourth dimension, it is magnifying all those emotions that need to be released; the thoughts and emotions, all the feelings of unworthiness, all the feelings of that which has dishonored and disrespected you. It is a dimension of balancing and what is occurring is a balancing within you and your body systems in order that you may vibrate at the fifth dimensional level, at ascension level, and this will keep on happening incrementally in order that it be a gradual and safe process.

Now, what is life like in the fifth dimension and how does one navigate one's self around it? In the fifth dimension, it is much like this fourth dimension. There are trees and flowers, birds and mountains, flora and fauna, and everything is very peaceful, harmonious, tranquil and sacred. One navigates here by understanding that your thoughts are powerful; it is what you envision in your mind as your intention that will bring you what you want, what you desire. All is in harmony, all is flowing in a peaceful manner and it really is most delightful, for here, you understand immediately that you are one with the Creator and you are creating all that you desire to bring to you instantly. That, of course, is a double edged sword; your mind must be balanced and disciplined and you must be aware that your creations are your personal responsibility. Your body will be of a higher, finer vibration in order to function and exist on the fifth dimension.

Your bodies at this time, as we pass through the fourth dimension, are being cleansed, transmuted and transformed, as you all know, and this will continue until there will come a point where you will be able to easily step into the fifth dimension in your finer, more purified body. There is a great Resurrection Dispensation from the Creator at the request of Lady Gaia/Mother Earth. She intends to ascend into the fifth dimension but she intends to do it by taking all of you with her.

It is a choice; a personal choice, that each of you make. Know that at the soul level, the majority of the world's population has made that choice. All of humanity wants to return to the Light and this is what is occurring. The fifth dimension is pristine, when you look at the leaves of trees; they are brilliant in their coloring. When you look at the flowers, they are vivid and alive, more so than ever upon the third or fourth dimension. Everything is much clearer, more vitally alive. When you step on the grass, it is alive and you know that it is alive, for it blesses you with love as you step upon it. It is a place of joy, peace and happiness. There are beautiful Temples; of Learning, of Healing, of Knowledge. There are all the positive experiences that you have ever desired upon the fifth dimension. It can all take place simply by your intention.

Train your mind to be balanced so that you always receive exactly what you want.

Look forward to great adventure in Creation and understand that this is why we are now focusing on you as a co-creator with the Divine, for this is what you have to be well versed in as you come into the higher dimensions of consciousness. Start now by creating what you *want*, the majority of you who read these words are already well on your way, for you are heeding the words of the Masters and you are honoring their requests and their advice, to guide you safely into the higher dimensions.

And it is not just you but all of your loved ones and all upon the Earth and indeed, the Earth herself. This will continue for quite some time, so make it an adventure, make a list of that which you desire and play with it as the creator that you really are. See what you want, write it down and decree it everyday for the highest good of all concerned. Play with these images and these thoughts to train your mind to be balanced so that you always receive exactly what you want.

This is a general overview of what you can expect as you step into the higher dimensions and what is happening at this time, so that you will have this knowledge and be secure in your thinking processes. This is occurring each day as you are raising your consciousness higher and higher. You are working so diligently to raise your frequency levels and it is having its positive effect.

Know that as you continue to do this, you are, in effect, ascending. Many of you are already almost through the fourth dimensional realm. Many of you are entering the fifth dimension and even further than that. You have done your work of clearing, you have looked at every dark aspect that was in you and have transmuted, balanced, released and integrated it. You are shining in your Glory! Know this, Dear Ones. Just keep on doing what you have been doing and you are and always will be, protected in this.

Now, when you reach the new dimension of consciousness, whichever one you have advanced to, you will find a world that may look a little bare to you, other than flora and fauna, mountains, lakes, and rivers and what you must understand, Dear Ones, is that you create your reality. Whatever you wish, you create it. If you wish to converse with another, if you wish to come see me and converse with me in my Retreat above the island of Crete, all you have to do is think it and you are with me. That is instant manifestation. This is what occurs in the higher planes, there is instant manifestation, so you must remember this.

We find it quite amusing at times, to watch the newcomers as they come into these higher dimensions, they create the most wondrous things, and it can be fun to observe…but we have many helpers here on this side of the veil who work specifically with the newcomers. Of course, as you are entering this new dimension, it is happening in greater numbers and will continue to be in greater numbers. That is why we are taking these steps now to teach you and make you aware and prepared for stepping into the higher dimensions.

There will be teams who greet you. Now, this depends on your awareness level. As you reach the higher planes, it is usually through the etheric levels and that might not necessarily come through to you in your physical body at this time. Know that as you reach within your consciousness to the higher levels, you are greeted by those whose purpose and task it is to welcome each newcomer. You really are not newcomers, Dear Ones, you do understand that. You are just returning to your natural state of being and, it does not really take that long for you to become acclimatized to your 'new' environment and you quickly choose where you wish to be of the greatest service.

Spiritual and soul growth doesn't stop when you reach the higher dimensions, it continues on.

In this dimension of existence, there is no time, and because of this, when you have eternity stretching before you, most souls want to fill that endlessness with purposeful activity, for spiritual and soul growth doesn't stop when you reach the higher dimensions, it continues on. The only difference is that now, you consciously choose your direction, your service and the reasons for this. It is always service to others that is chosen. It is always service in some way, whether you choose to serve those you have left behind on the Earth plane, who need assistance to rise to this level, and this is where most of you have and will make that choice to be of service; but there are other choices, other planetary assignments, other areas where you can be of assistance, the higher that you go on the dimensional levels.

All of this is known to you as the Eternal Self that you are and you quickly assume your new roles and move towards them. Many of you, after lifetimes of struggle and toil, choose to just BE and enjoy all that

30

you would wish to enjoy, that which you never gave yourself time for or did not have time for, upon the Earth plane and so you do this for a time, and since there is no time, that could be like ages upon the Earth plane as it exists now.

You are the Way Showers - as the bridge between the two dimensions.

There is an unlimited variety of areas and activities that you may enter into, and so, it is not a void that you come into; it is a lively world with great activity. If you wish to learn the Mastery of manifestation, or the Mastery of teaching another, the Mastery of Healing, the Mastery of working with Light, the Mastery of working with energies, it is all here for you to learn and do. There are Temples where you can learn these methods; there are Teachers who are well versed in these disciplines who are available to give you instruction. There is no payment for this. The payment that the Teachers receive for this is in terms of their own soul advancement, for that is how the higher dimensions operate. It is service for the purpose of advancing your own soul into higher frequency so this just continues on. All of you know this and will remember this as you reach this level.

There is much enjoyment here and this dimension is filled with activities such as singing and dancing, group activities, plays, music...it is all very delightful! Know that life here is vibrant and free, for you have but to think of what it is that you want to experience and you are in it.

Now, Dear Ones, the bridges to this dimension are being created and you are being drawn to those bridges, and you know this also, deep within your hearts. You are being led to these bridges by your Divine self and so, your work has begun in earnest. There is a Great Work happening upon this world now between the dimensions and you are the Way Showers - as the bridge between the two dimensions. There is much activity taking place. There are many new openings happening and being created, each day. As you are raised higher through your disciplines, whether it be meditation, decreeing, visualization, or imagination, it is you who are creating these bridges between the dimensions. As you persist in your spiritual disciplines and blaze your trails, know that many others now have a path of Light to follow in your wake. You are creating a great blessing for others by doing your work of raising your consciousness to the highest dimensions.

You must change the pathways, and the way to do this is through persistent and consistent efforts, to concentrate on that which you want.

Continue on, creating your dreams and making your visions manifest within your lives, within the Earth reality. This is something that is challenging for many of you, as your focus is always usurped by the needs of the hour, by the needs of the moment, by your responsibilities in your daily Earthly lives to your self and others and to your 'shoulds', 'must have's' and 'must do's'.

In order to make your dreams come true, to make your dreams a reality, you have to find, first of all, the focus. Take the time to sit down and write down what your goals, your desires and your dreams truly are. Once you have done this, and you refine this list, find the appropriate affirmations and decrees that will enable you to bring this about into manifestation in your daily lives. This requires dedication and persistence. It requires that you set your intentions in a plan to make your dreams manifest, and to 'work' your plan. It requires for you to do this in a persistent manner so that you may acquire new neural pathways in your brain, so that all the mental and emotional conditioning from your life to this point, is overcome. You must change the pathways, and the way to do this is through persistent and consistent efforts, to concentrate on that which you *want*.

We, your Family of Light, understand that this is a difficult challenge for you, because you have responsibilities to your husbands or wives, to your children, your grandchildren, to your extended biological family members, to others… but, it is very important to make the time for yourselves! Realize the importance of developing yourselves, and as you do this, you will realize that all those 'have to's, 'should's', and 'must's', begin to align themselves to your new vision. Before you know it, everything unfolds before you in grace and ease. With this come the most miraculous synchronicities and assistance from On High. All that is required of you is to persist, to focus first on what it is that you want to accomplish or manifest in your reality and then persist each day, several times a day. When you first begin to do this, you may have to do this every spare moment, and the more that you persist and do this, the easier it will become and before you know it, it is a joy and a pleasure to do this each day. As you do this, you will notice your life unfolding and flowing in the most of harmonious of ways.

Focus first on what it is that you want to accomplish or manifest in your reality and then persist each day.

It is very important to honor your own needs. Know that this is one of the requirements for Ascension, for in order to ascend to a higher consciousness, you have to be able to manifest and create your own reality. No one else will do this for you, Dear Ones. You must do this for yourself. Know this and take note of the method that I have given, for it is a safe and sure method, a persistent and consistent method of achieving your goals. We are speedily entering a new reality where each of you will be called upon to create that which you require, that which you desire, and it behooves you to put into practice now that which will be the most helpful in the times that are ahead.

Know that when you call upon we, of the higher dimensions, that you are instantly assisted. You may not see this or feel this, but it is so. You are surrounded by great beings of Light. You always have assistance; you always have spiritual helpers and friends who are always at your side. The Guides that you have chosen and who have agreed to walk with you every day upon this Earth are always with you and new ones are assigned to you as you progress in raising your consciousness to higher levels.

You are precious to the Family of Light and we will do all in our strength and power to bring you assistance.

Call upon them; ask for their guidance and inspiration. When you feel down about things, call upon your Guides, the Angels and Archangels to come to you and uplift your spirits. It happens so quickly and subtly, that before you know it, you find yourself in higher spirits, on a higher mental and emotional plane. It is very important at this time to maintain a balance within yourselves, so do call upon your Guides, call upon the Angels, call upon the Masters and Lady Masters, for we are here at this time to specifically help each of you. We can 'hang around' you but if you do not ask us specifically for the assistance that you require at every moment, we can only surround you with our love.

Know that you and each of your beloved family members, your biological family members, are always surrounded and protected in all ways. If any of your family members are going through difficulties, call upon us to give them assistance, for *you* are their bridge between Heaven and Earth. This is a role that you agreed to play in this lifetime for them and they are blessed to have your presence in their lives because you are great lightning rods upon this world. You instantly attract all the assistance that you request for yourselves and for your beloved family members. These are some of the benefits of being a dedicated Lightworker at this time on planet Earth. Do not hesitate to call upon us if you find yourself or your family members in such circumstances.

We are here to serve you, this is the work that we have chosen, this is how we serve our Creator, so please, Dear Ones, put us to use in this way. You have become so used to going within trying to connect with your inner strength that you sometimes forget about the resources that you have on hand, simply for the asking. Do remember this, Dear Ones. We are here to give you assistance whenever it is needed. You are loved beyond measure. You are precious to we of the higher dimensions and we will do all in our strength and power to bring you assistance.

I would like to return to my discourse on what you, the Lightworkers, and those who walk the path of Light and the path of Ascension into higher consciousness can expect to find upon the higher dimensions. As spiritual beings, everything that happens on the higher dimensions is directly related to your creative manifesting ability. That includes all…everything, it includes the mode of dress, the mode of appearance, even the color of your hair and your eyes. All of this is as *you* create and manifest. We see many beings who come into this dimension experimenting, by having different colored hair, different colored eyes, or taking on the forms from different lifetimes. All of this is possible, all here can be made manifest and created as perfection.

Clothing is also created, even designed, according to each being's will and desire. The colors that they wear are the outer manifestation of the being and what they wish to manifest at each moment. There is much color here, a great variety of colors in clothing and robes, we do not just walk around in white robes as we are depicted by the people of Earth on the third and fourth dimension, although we do have and wear white robes. It is all a matter of personal choice. The mode of clothing is loose and comfortable with intricate designs…embroidery, jewels, beads, of decoration. Each being here loves to shine in all their glory and it is all possible here. We have a great time imaging and creating the robes and clothing, the jewels and gems that we wish to appear in at any moment.

A lot of us who belong to certain Orders wear the colors associated with that Order, for an example, those who belong to the Order of

Melchizedek wear white robes with gold embroideries, golden jewelry, golden gemstones. All is beautiful and perfect. There are other Orders who wear the color orange, the color pink, the color blue, the color green, the color yellow, there are the robes of that Order. There is a great variety and everything is a riot of vibrant color.

All great constructive and beneficial ideas come from the higher dimensions as a gift from those who wish to bless their sisters and brothers with greater Light and love.

When souls ascend to the higher dimensions, they immediately set about creating perfection in their forms that they were unhappy with upon the Earth such as, crookedness of teeth and they immediately create perfection…beautiful, shining, gleaming, pearly white teeth, and this practice of creation continues in every way. All forms are beautiful and perfect here.

There is much less density and as the beings here wish to see someone else or travel some place else, it is all accomplished through the mind. What their mind can conceive on this higher plane of existence, the being can achieve, so this is of delight to those who are newly come to the higher dimensions, for it is wonderful for them to rediscover the grace and ease of our Prime Creator's Divine abundance. Everything each soul could ever desire is provided instantly, is manifested instantly. If someone wishes to eat a pear, the pear appears in their hand, whole and perfect, delicious, succulent, juicy and sweet. The flavor is beyond anything ever imagined on the Earth plane. All is perfection, and that includes taste, sight and sound. All is harmonious and joyful. Creation is always joyfully creating. Much creation occurs and as each is wanted and desired, a soul merely has to picture in their minds what it is that they wish and they *are* that.

There are higher and higher levels on the higher dimensions so one continuously gives of oneself in service in order to progress up the higher levels. Most beings of a certain frequency congregate and manifest on a certain level in groups. As their frequency, awareness, the amount of service and the purity of intent is increased, the greater the levels to which one aspires becomes possible. Each being finds other beings of like vibration and frequency up through all the levels. There are an infinite number of levels of manifestation in the higher dimensions. It is a world rich and vibrant with life at every level. Much is revealed as one's progress moves up through the levels of frequencies.

This is the most loving Dispensation that has ever been given to humanity.

Each soul is able to traverse the levels of frequency and vibration that they have aspired to, and can also maintain a connection with those on the Earth plane so that one never loses contact with one's friends or family members that may still be incarnated on Earth. It is all a matter of awareness and one can simply intend where they wish to be and they are immediately there. That is not the case with traversing up through the higher levels, for one must earn their way in this regard by being of service to our Beloved Creator, to the Light. That is why I stress the importance of being of service, for this is how one on the higher levels of existence progresses into the higher and higher levels.

Many beings here like to create great beauty in the form of new species of plants, flowers and trees, and they experiment enthusiastically to create beautiful vistas for others to enjoy on their frequency level. There is much 'daily', what you would call 'daily' since there is no time here, activity with those who are pursuing their educational interests where they take up training in the healing disciplines, in the sciences and the arts, in the implementation of new methods that help to create greater Light in all of the dimensions, and there is much knowledge of new inventions that is imparted, and these conceptions are then filtered down upon the Earth levels.

The souls on Earth who are open to these new ideas see the entire plan in their mind's eye and have the knowledge of its workings given to them so that they can create new inventions, technologies or modalities, works of art or healing methods. All great constructive and beneficial ideas come from the higher dimensions as a gift from those who wish to bless their sisters and brothers with greater Light and love. This is what is meant by the saying, 'As above, so below', for those above who have stepped off the re-incarnational cycle always turn and give a hand to those below who are in physical incarnation on Earth and that is true sisterhood and brotherhood.

We will address the meaning of the words 'Resurrection Dispensation'. Now, 'dispensation' is a Grace from Creator. That is what a 'dispensation' is, it is permission if you like, from Creator that was petitioned for and granted. Many Ascended Masters from the spiritual Family of Light petitioned on behalf of humanity for the 'Resurrection' Dispensation. What was asked for by the Family of Light was for humanity to be granted a 'clean slate' as they work upon clearing and purging in their current lifetimes so that they are no longer required to work through lifetime after lifetime of karma. In order for humanity to ascend with the Earth, it was deemed appropriate that this Dispensation be granted so that the Divine Plan can take as many of humanity with the Earth as possible. This was granted by Prime Creator.

What this means is the requirement to balance and clear all of one's karma has been lifted. All that is required now is that each human being clears a minimum of 51% of previous karma. That means that one is not required to continue endlessly in this endeavour which would require many, many, more lifetimes, and they would not be able to take advantage of this great and wonderful opportunity for ascension with the Earth into the higher dimensions during these times. This, of course, does not totally free humanity so that they go and continue to create more karma. It is a Sacred Gift; one that each should honor as the Sacred Opportunity that it is, offered at this time in the history of the Earth. This is the most loving Dispensation that has ever been given to humanity. It has facilitated much movement in the frequency levels of humanity, for now, most humans upon this Earth are being cleared and can move forward by raising their frequency levels through the various spiritual disciplines and working diligently to bring themselves to Ascension levels.

Uplift the Earth into the higher dimensions that she may become the shining Star that is her destiny.

There are many ways this can be done. There are, for instance, Activators who work through seminars or the telephone and conferencing systems who work in unison with the Ascended Masters and even, the Galactic Masters, to infuse those who participate, with higher frequency levels and also DNA activations and this is very, very helpful. It gives each person who participates the boost that they need. It also means the person who participates in these seminars, telephone conference calls or webinars, also needs to work on themselves in between the calls in order to keep that frequency at its raised level. It is not a 'free ride', Dear Ones. One must apply themselves each and every day. This is where your decreeing comes in as one way to do this and this is why it is so important.

Many of you like to maintain your frequency levels by listening to music which activates and raises your vibratory level. This is, for the most part, beautiful, harmonious music that has been created for this purpose and to which you resonate. You know which music and sound vibration is of high benefit to you. If you fall into this category, continue on, for it is a tool that is working for you. As the years go on, there will be more and more sound activations taking place upon the Earth plane, for this is a universal way that encompasses the use of mathematical formulas that can activate people's DNA in a very swift manner which can encompass all of humanity. This is what is coming forth now and it will continue to do so as the years into the new Golden Age progress.

Those of you who choose and resonate with meditation have always found this an excellent means of not only centering and balancing yourselves but also raising your frequency levels. This is a tried and true method to do so.

There is also a path of service to others, for this discipline also raises one's frequency level and trains and teaches the person who uses this path to think of others rather than self. It is a means of denouncing all worldly things and working for the greater and highest good of all concerned. This is what Mother Theresa did and the path she used to gain Ascension into the higher frequency levels, the higher dimensions. This path of service is open to all, and many more could choose it as a means to increasing their frequency levels. It is all a matter of choice.

The path of decreeing is also one of these paths. Decreeing is a discipline which trains one's voice, one's mind, one's heart, one's soul, all parts of their being to see themselves as the powerful creator beings that they are. Each day that one pursues this discipline raises one's frequency vibration; those who decree daily can vouch for this, for the energies that run through people who daily decree is at a very high level.

What is also available for you is that you can call upon the Ascended Masters to work with you and when you do this, it greatly accelerates your progress in raising your frequency levels. Do remember, Dear Ones, there are so many Ascended Masters who are willing and eager to give you assistance. Call upon us, work with us. We will work with you daily and nightly to raise you to ascension levels. Know that this is a joy for us to do, it is not an imposition. It is a joy for us to serve you in this way and we ask you to use all of these methods to consecrate yourself to your upliftment into the higher dimensions of consciousness, to uplift the Earth into the higher dimensions that she may become the shining Star that is her destiny. Each of you is a shining Star also as you raise your frequency levels to the highest dimensions that you could attain each day. As you continue to do this, your frequency levels continue to radiate higher and higher.

It requires dedication, it requires work on your part but know that you have been granted the greatest gift in the Resurrection Dispensation.

It behooves each of you to feel gratitude for this great opportunity that has been granted to all of humanity upon the Earth. We continue to work with you; we continue to give you our timely advice, and words of encouragement and upliftment to keep you firmly on your path of Ascension.

- Chapter 3 -
The Time is Now!

I wish to discourse with you on your growing and developing extrasensory abilities. What is occurring with the high intensity energies on the Earth plane at this time is creating not only some discomfort for you in your bodies but also in your energy bodies which surround you. As your Divine Self is calibrating and integrating within your auric field, more of your talents and abilities are being brought to the surface. There is already, as you have noticed, many new channelers who are bringing forth messages from the higher planes of existence and the opening of these gifts within more people shall continue in the days ahead.

There will also be many of you who will be receiving plans, codes and information to bring through new technologies, so we from the Family of Light are informing you that this is beginning to occur. As we have mentioned once before, we require willingness and intention on your part, so you must state each day that you are willing to receive these. Do call upon us and we will endeavor to work with you to bring through new healing knowledge and modalities, new knowledge and information that is ancient beyond memory. It is now ready to come upon your world again, to move humanity into the most wonderful, exciting Era, the new Golden Age.

Once you ask us (remember to do this each day) be prepared to be inspired at the most inopportune times. You must realize when it starts to come through you, that this is the energy and information being given from the higher realms.

It is advisable that you carry a notepad and pen with you and keep it near to you at all times. By doing this, you can record the ideas and flashes of inspiration that come to you. Once you receive them, you must act upon them, for an idea that sits in someone's mind or upon a piece of paper that is not acted upon will not come forth to bless your world or will perhaps be acted upon by another!

Spend some time each day imagining what you would like to bring into this new world and ask for it. There is so much activity that is occurring on our planes of existence at this time. You who are decreeing are keeping us gainfully occupied, and there is much that is being accomplished throughout your world in answer to your specific decrees. So do keep on keeping on, Dear Ones. We will continue to answer your calls, for you have answered *our* calls and we are now working in unity with you and it is a joy and a pleasure for us to do so. We are in partnership, and it feels wonderful to have this two way communication that is occurring between the Family of Light and you, in your rising consciousness and awareness.

"I am ready to receive new information from the Christed Light realms that will bless the Earth and all upon her, for the highest good of all concerned. So it is done!"

I remind you to be prepared for an influx of information, a flash of inspiration, or an idea for a new painting or other creative project that appears in your mind's eye, or a poem, or other creative ideas that come into your awareness in a flash. There will be visions of new books to be written, new knowledge to come forth. You it is, who will bring them forth. Know this and prepare yourselves. Let us know if you are willing to receive this information, just state "I am ready to receive new information from the Christed Light realms that will bless the Earth and all upon her, for the highest good of all concerned. So it is done!" and then, be open to receive.

There are great energetic openings occurring throughout the world as you practice your decreeing, your affirmations, or your meditations. These influences are beginning to spread ever wider across the surface of the Earth, and this is in the Divine Plan. It is an amazing sight to behold. The Earth so dearly wants all upon her to come with her into the higher dimensions and is so grateful for all that you are doing to keep her stabilized. She has sacrificed so much that this may occur in harmony and in unison with each human being, in unison with all the kingdoms upon the Earth. You are all One. Call upon the Earth to work with you, for in this way there is communication from Father Sky and Mother Earth and this is the balance that is required and needed to see the Earth and all upon her through the coming days. Do this in a spirit of joy, do this in a spirit of service, for it is of the higher realms to be in service to the Light and we rejoice at those who perform this service in answer to our Calls.

The energies and alignments in the cosmos that are happening now are auspicious to gain greater benefit for you and the rest of humanity.

I would like to speak with you about what is meant by the term "The Time is Now". What we of the Family of Light mean when we say that to you, is that the energies and alignments in the cosmos that are happening now are auspicious to gain greater benefit for you and the rest of humanity, and so it is important to focus on that which you want.

There is, right now, great movement happening within the Earth, on the Earth and around the Earth. There is energy going into every space and place within each person, within the Earth herself and it is bringing up many energies, most especially within people, at this time. This will continue in increasing intensity so you who respond when we say "The Time is Now" - you bring in the great stabilizing energies - for it is the grounding of your Light into the center of the Earth's core, the crystalline core, that blesses Mother Earth, who then in turn stabilizes and radiates this blessing outwards within the regions of her Inner Self and upon her surface, and even in the weather patterns.

All is inter-related - all is One. The energies that are being processed, expressed and manifested through humanity at this time are coming through at a great rate. As all that needs to be released takes place, there also needs to be grounding of the cosmic Light to keep the Earth in a more stable place. There are many areas upon the planet that are manifesting these energies at this time and it is very important that we get as many of you upon the Earth to work with us in this way.

For the very first time in the Earth's long history, humanity as a whole has the opportunity to rise into the higher dimensions.

Also the term, "The Time is Now" refers to this most wondrous time in the history of the Earth, this graduation, if you will, from the lower dimensions into the higher, more refined dimensions of life and living. For the very first time in the Earth's long history, humanity as a whole has the opportunity to rise into the higher dimensions in their physical bodies, albeit a more refined and cleansed, light filled body. This has never occurred anywhere in the universe before.

There are many who are participating in the etheric realms to help bring this about. When their assistance is called upon by you of the Earth, this gives them the opportunity to step in and add their considerable power and energy to bring this about. Whether you remember in your waking consciousness what we are working together on or not, be assured that we do consult together upon the etheric planes while your physical bodies sleep and we know each new step and work together to accomplish these projects. The Great Light that is being streamed to the Earth from the Great Central Sun at Galactic center is very powerful in its intensity and has to be 'stepped down' as it were, in order for humanity to absorb, assimilate and integrate these energies. There is a great cooperation in unity and purpose that is occurring from our planes of existence and the Earth planes of existence with each person who is willing to be of assistance in this way. As you become aware that this is occurring, more of you become willing in the higher levels to take on this task to assist us in this way. There is much that is being accomplished, but there is still much Great Work that has to be done, so therefore, the time is now, Dear Ones, the time for the work that has to be done is at hand.

Open yourselves up to embrace all that lives in your field of possibilities. One has only to open their minds, their thinking and indicate their willingness to be open to all the possibilities within their field of potential and then be in joyous anticipation. Those wonderful fields of possibilities begin to anchor into your being and to become part of your personal experience.

Open yourselves up to embrace all that lives in your field of possibilities.

Life on Earth at this time is filled with great possibilities, Dear Ones. It requires you to move 'outside the box' of where your thinking processes have taken you in a well-beaten path throughout your lifetime. It is time to step outside that box and off that path and open up to new ideas and new thoughts. When this occurs, the world opens up those new ideas, new thoughts, new energies to you, and you become then, the manifestor of newness, that which will inhabit your new world.

It is a difficult task to move past the well-beaten paths that you have tread upon for your entire life upon this Earth but if you can, just for a few moments each day, step into the realm of all that is possible for you and for your new world, miracles will take place. There is, on the brink of the enlightening of the people of Earth, much knowledge that is seeded in the new energies that are streaming upon the Earth at this time. All that is required is to be open and willing to receive this knowledge and to state this willingness each day. The changes that are about to take place will take place through each and every one of you! Open yourselves to all these possibilities, open yourselves by stating that you are willing to step off your well-beaten paths to something new and it shall be so.

In the days ahead more of these possibilities will be brought to the Earth by those who stepped off their well-beaten paths and embraced the possibilities of the new, and the opportunity it provided. There is a new world birthing, Dear Ones; all that is required of you is to open yourself up. Clear your energy fields each day and set your sights on the new possibilities to create your new world, a world filled with excitement, a world that goes beyond all limitations of the old paradigm.

There is, on the brink of the enlightening of the people of Earth, much knowledge that is seeded in the new energies that are streaming upon the Earth.

There will be much that is new and exciting that will be brought to the forefront by those who are open, willing and awake to the fact that these energies exist. You it is, who will be the pioneers, the inventors, the creators of the *new*. All that is given will come to those who have proven themselves as those who embrace the Light for the highest good of all concerned. Leave all preconceived notions behind you and just be open to what can come through. I, Hilarion, am feeling very hopeful and excited by that which is being filtered down upon the Earth plane at this time, to be absorbed and embraced by those who are ready and willing to be engaged in this way.

I will work with every one who calls upon me. Knowledge comes forth, knowledge that was once hidden, knowledge that was suppressed from those upon the Earth, knowledge of inventions and technology that was prevented from coming into manifestation in the world and making a real difference. Those days are now upon us and they can no longer be suppressed. They will be given to those who ask, to those whose hearts are true and pure; those who have agreed to play this role at this momentous time in the history of the world. As the days into the new Golden Age continue, there will be wondrous new technology, knowledge and inventions being brought forth. There is already much that is new waiting to be announced, waiting for the people of Earth to discover its existence.

Make a habit each day of doing Google searches for new technology and you will be amazed at what you find! Go forward, become excited, reaching with your minds toward the stars, for the stars are endless in a sea of infinite possibilities! As you open and move past your previous human conditioning, you will begin to experience the wonder of life in a human body, the wonder of your own great Divine Self, the joy of manifesting in a physical body. This in itself is a wonder to behold, a wonder and a great honor to be experiencing…for many beings stood in line to be where you are now but it was you that was chosen. That is a miracle, that it is *you* that is here at this time bringing forth the wonders into your new world. The new world is like a blank slate and can be filled with every good thing, and you are playing the roles of the creators of it. Move forward, and create; you are receiving so many new ideas and assistance, and all that is required of you is to be willing to seize the moment and create the miracles that will be commonplace in your new world in just a few more years. Go forth, pioneers of the new reality, go forth and blaze your trails of Light, of love, for the highest good of all!

You it is, who will be the pioneers, the inventors, the creators of the new.

Know that from these moments on, *you* are the blessing of humanity. YOU are the Emissaries of Light in all ways and that which comes through you will bless many, many, many generations to come. The Divine Feminine energies are streaming down and carry the impetus of great creativity. Seize the moment, Dear Ones, seize the moment!

I wish to bring to your attention the need that you have at this time which is, the need to honor yourselves. There are many 'other' energies that are impinging upon your own; family commitments, family emergencies, family concerns that are coming fast and furious with their needs into your lives. What is necessary is to not resist this but to go with the flow and experience the moments and do what must be done. Know that your spiritual progress will continue on. If it is possible for you to say a few of your decrees each day to keep your energies up, that is all that is required. It is a commitment to yourselves, for when your energies are high, all in your daily life flows as it should. Remember this as you rise to meet the needs of your families, and of others.

Events throughout the world are continuing in their intensity to move into the areas of consciousness that gives all people the opportunity to look with clarity upon their issues, upon that which is ready to be released and transmuted and this will continue to occur as the days go on. When one does not resist what is occurring but flows with the moment and the need, it is not as difficult as it might seem. It is after all, what one's attitude is that is important in these moments.

Go forward; become excited, reaching with your mind toward the stars, for the stars are endless in a sea of infinite possibilities!

At times in your lives when you make great commitments to yourselves, to raise your frequency levels and to move forward in your spiritual progress, there seems to be a law that comes into effect with events, people, and happenings which seem to prevent you from accomplishing your great purpose, and this is a sort of test that occurs. It is as though the 'others' sense your new and great purpose and they rush in to fill your space. This is a part of the family grids, the mass consciousness grids and those who are Lightworker's find this very challenging and yet, because of family commitments, caring and love of the 'other', naturally enough, Lightworker's will choose to give of themselves to their family. So what I am telling you, Dear Ones, is; do not beat yourselves up because your plans are not working out. When the timing is right, all of this will flow and work beautifully.

This 'in between' time of movement through the fourth dimension into the fifth, is a trying place to be, for you have one foot in each dimension. Being the 'bridge' between both dimensions can be very challenging at times. As you have been diligently working through all your issues, it now seems that you are also working through the issues of

49

your loved ones, friends, and families. That is the role that you chose because of your great love for those who are in your immediate family, your biological family members and your friends. It was your great desire to play this role in their life in order to help them with their issues, giving freely of your love and compassion. As their great needs are presented to you, just allow yourself to respond to them naturally.

Many Beings stood in line to be where you are now but it was you that was chosen!

As you continue on your road to self mastery, to become the Masters of your world, you will find it challenging in these ways. There is no longer those places or spaces in your world where you can 'retire' from the world until you have gained your Mastery as was possible in the days of old, for in the days of old, those of us who gained our self mastery, who became Masters of Life in the physical, were only able to do so by withdrawing from the world at large for great amounts of time. We look upon each of you who are faced with these challenges of devoting the time necessary to create Mastery within yourselves and yet, still meet the needs of your families and those around you and we applaud you, support you and honor you.

Know that we are always available to you in these times, call upon us by requesting our assistance, our upliftment and guidance as necessary. We will do all in our power to give you that assistance, that upliftment and help you stay steadfast on your great purpose. In your great desire to regain your Mastery you have only to intend it and you will be given the assistance from us; for example, in the form of suddenly finding the space of time needed in order to accomplish what you wish to accomplish, to go within and remember who you truly are and why you came to the Earth and you will have the opportunity to do that. These new energies are working first on the immediate members of your family and friends, and as you respond to their needs and minister to them so that their needs are met, then you will have the space that you need to devote your energies to your forward movement. In the infinite scheme of things, there is all the time in the world to accomplish your tasks.

We thank you for your devotion and your steadfastness in the wake of all the demands upon your time at this juncture of transformation. We honor and appreciate each and every one of you.

That is your great task at this time, Dear Ones, to maintain the stability of the Earth and everyone upon the Earth.

I wish to speak to you now about all of the increasing, intensified energies that are streaming down upon the Earth. As this is occurring, much cleansing is taking place for much that has been stored within is being uncovered that was hidden before, within every man, woman and child upon the Earth, and within all of the workings of all of the institutions upon the Earth. Many, many of you have been literally reduced to lying in a prone position as these energies have been coming forth and this is actually a good thing, Dear Ones, for then you are resting and you are integrating the new energies. The need to increase the frequency level or at least maintain it every day is of prime importance at this time, for these energies are ever increasing in their intensity and one must rise and meet them.

I would like to recommend that before you start your daily disciplines, that you ask and intend that your frequency level be doubled from the day before in safety, grace and ease. This will help you immensely in the raising of your frequency levels and might give assistance to you in assimilating and integrating these new energies.

Behind the scenes in your world there is much that has been taking place and much that will be coming forth in the days directly ahead of you. There are great changes and revelations that are going to be revealed, and these will change the face of the Earth. They will change the attitudes of all the people upon the Earth and will change the way

51

that people have been thinking. As this process occurs, much Light will radiate with more intensity upon the Earth plane and this is highly desirable. At the same time, as these energies create this change within each person, it will be a difficult transformation for many. We ask you to remain in your center, stay balanced and keep up the stability of the Earth and everyone upon it by being stable within your own system. That is your great task at this time, Dear Ones, to maintain the stability of the Earth and everyone upon it.

One needs to be very adaptable and flexible in the events taking place.

There has literally been a shift in the Earth. Those of you who have compasses may check this out, you will find something very surprising has occurred and as you can see, the Great Shift has occurred without disaster of any kind. It is now full speed ahead, the way forward has been clearing and all that remains is the completion of the cleansing and purifying and the revealing of all that was hidden before. Each day in every way, Beloved Ones, be the Light, stand in your Light, radiate your Light, your compassion, your love, tolerance and patience, for now, your sisters and brothers are beginning to go through the changes that you have already experienced and have almost completed. Remember to turn back and lend a hand wherever you see that it is necessary.

This is the time of many strange revelations, of many strange happenings on the Earth and around the Earth, and in the atmosphere. One needs to be very adaptable and flexible in the events taking place. It is important to maintain and cultivate the feeling of joy and happy expectation and to picture the end result of what it is that you have all desired to accomplish. All is working according to the Divine Plan for the highest good of all concerned and there remains now the completion of all that is necessary to release, remove and let go of. This is so that you all, along with your sisters and brothers and Mother Earth, can sail into the new Dimension, the New Golden Age. It is not only a consciousness shift that is occurring but also the physical shift of the Earth. It behooves everyone to become aware of this.

There will be a 'forgetfulness' of the old paradigm, the old ways of thinking, being and doing, and in its place will come true loving kindness, true helpfulness, true sisterhood and brotherhood between all the people of the Earth.

You have been prepared, tested and tried and have emerged victorious!

We of the higher dimensions along with the galactic sisters and brothers have been working unceasingly while you have been assimilating and integrating the new energies. Not only have we been assisting you, we have also been collectively directing balancing energies wherever they are needed the most to keep everything stabilized, to keep everything on an even keel. There is much good coming for the people of Earth, much that is positive and beneficial, that is a blessing for all of humanity everywhere. As all the people of the Earth are blessed, so too, is the Earth blessed, for you and all of Creation are One. We are going into greater unity consciousness now and the thinking process within every human being upon the Earth is changing and will continue to change. There will be a 'forgetfulness' of the old paradigm, the old ways of thinking, being and doing, and in its place will come true loving kindness, true helpfulness, true sisterhood and brotherhood between all the people of the Earth.

This will be a gradual process; it will not be something that happens instantly but rather incrementally every day. There will be some noticeable changes and those who are aware will notice those changes. Each person is now being called upon to step into their mission, the task that they chose to take part in as their part of the Divine Plan before they came to the Earth at this moment in history. You have been prepared, tested and tried and have emerged victorious, Dear Ones. Now you have the opportunity to step into your roles as the teachers and guides, as the

Masters of Life in the physical. If you are not yet cognizant of what your role in all of this is, just relax, Dear Ones, for it shall come to you as easily and naturally as breathing in the days ahead. For you who have been working so diligently, your remembrance processes are being stepped up so that you will come into full remembrance and begin to implement and put into action, your part of the Divine Plan.

Truly, this is an amazing, wondrous and miraculous time to manifest upon the Earth and we look upon you with great pride, knowing that soon, our part in the Divine Plan will be complete, and we shall move forward into the next step of our journey. This has been a true labor of love by all those in the Ascended Light Realms. By no means, is the job finished and complete. A major portion of it has been the task of awakening the beloved Lightworkers, who volunteered to come to the Earth with complete amnesia so that they could be in their human forms upon the Earth when these great events and changes start to occur. Hold the vision of the new Earth in your minds and in your hearts; see the world that you want with all of your Being. Strongly intend that peace, harmony and the Light prevail upon the Earth.

- Chapter 4 -
The Inner Changes Taking Place

All Beings are adding their energies, whether it be in magnification of the energies that you are creating each day or whether it be through giving personal assistance to each person who requires it or whether it be in unison with the higher realms. Know that every soul, incarnate or discarnate, is working earnestly to bring Heaven on Earth in grace, ease and protection, in its highest, fullest potential and manifestation. This work continues and we are filled with gratitude at all of your opened hearts and your willingness to be a part of this great effort. We are filled with so much love and gratitude to each of you, that you are remembering the reason that you came to the Earth during these times. There was no guarantee before you came that you would remember, but you did remember, you are remembering, and it gratifying to all of us who have worked so hard to make these moments manifest upon the Earth plane.

Know that you are being blessed beyond measure each and every day of your lives upon the Earth. Please realize how precious you are to Prime Creator, to the higher dimensions of life. You are so precious…beautiful, precious jewels. Hold that image within your minds and hearts and continue your great, selfless, loving service to humanity, the Earth and all upon her.

I wish to speak to you about methods that you may use to more quickly and easily release emotions and feelings of the old paradigm of polarity and duality. It requires that you state your intention each day as you release whatever comes up for you, that you release it and refill what you have released, and the resultant space that is available, with the liquid golden cosmic Christ Light. This will ensure that no other negativity will take the place of that which you have released. Use this method, Dear Ones, every time negativity surfaces and any old 'unresolved issues' surface. There is much at this time that is coming up from within you.

This is a very healthy process, for this process needs to be done before humanity as a whole can continue on into higher consciousness. All that holds you back from spiritual freedom must be released, and so I just wanted to remind you that by stating your intention, by stating your forgiveness of the person or situation involved and your intention to release it and then stating that you intend that what you released be replaced by the liquid golden cosmic Christ Light. This will be very, very beneficial to every one of you.

There is no escape from this for anyone. All is being brought up, all that has been hidden within people's minds, hearts and emotions is coming to the surface to be transmuted and released.

There are a lot of situations upon the Earth plane at this time that are rather bizarre and so we ask you to not become enmeshed in the dramas that are unfolding. There is much that is being released on community levels, city levels, national levels, continent levels. All is being released, purged and cleansed throughout the world in every place and space, and in its stead, comes the great Cosmic Light, in its stead, purity takes hold, in its stead, peace and harmony vibrate, in its stead, love prevails. Little by little each day, through the coming weeks, months and years, the Earth and everyone upon the Earth is being purified in this manner. There is no escape from this for anyone. All is being brought up, all that has been hidden within people's minds and hearts and emotions is coming to the surface to be transmuted and released, for forgiveness to take place, for the Light of the cosmic Christ to take its place and refill those places and spaces.

There is much activity upon the Earth plane in this regard and it can be a process that one can project humor into when one is going through the releasing of grief, sorrow and sadness, of feelings of betrayal, feelings of not being loved and not being worthy. As all these emotions and old conditionings come up for your awareness, state your intention to release and let go and forgive, and then make it a game, replace it with a new vision of what you truly want to create in your new life. Do not let yourself wallow in what you are releasing, recognize that it is old energy that is coming forth to be recycled, transmuted and renewed. If you do this and take on joy, happiness and a feeling of playfulness through those tears that you shed, great good can be accomplished within you.

Remember, the utmost priority of each and every one of you is Ascension!

As the world and all of humanity release all that has not been brought to the Light and resolved, it is creating new opportunities for bringing in greater visions, greater potentials and greater possibilities for all. However, you must claim them, you must intend them; you must rise above self pity, you must rise above the old programs that are surfacing within you. Rise above them and set a new priority. Remember, the utmost priority of each and every one of you is *Ascension*. For you who are reading this, it is your *Ascension Lifetime* and that should be of prime priority in your minds and intentions. Remember this, Dear Ones, this is why you are here at this time. Of course, that is not the only reason that you are here, for you are also here to ensure that those who are not as strong in the Light as you, are assisted in raising their own frequency levels to a higher space and place. So your purpose here on Earth serves many higher purposes as well.

In this moment of Now upon the Earth, there is, beyond the apparent purging and cleansing, a feeling pervading the hearts and minds of all humanity and it is the feeling of hope, the feeling of greater miracles that are soon to come into being and we ask you to hold on to those feelings. You are in fact, responding to the greater energies that are bringing cosmic love energies and a higher vibration and frequency to all upon the Earth and to the Earth. So encourage this by participating in this process in a *conscious* manner, by creating more feelings of joy, happiness and gratitude. These emotions are so very helpful at this time, to keep you focused on that which is important and the reason why you have come to the Earth plane.

Refrain from being caught up in negative dramas that are occurring everywhere at this time.

Soon, in your terms of soon, in linear time, there will come revelations and events that will create such joy within the hearts of humanity that it will automatically raise the level of vibration of the entire planet in just moments. It has happened before, when Lightworkers were filled with joy at the thought of a true first contact with the beloved galactic brothers and sisters that would be visible for all upon the Earth to see. By the anticipation of this great event, the Earth frequency level was raised and humanity was blessed by this raised frequency level. All upon the Earth are in a different place and space because of it. That is why I have brought up what has occurred in the your recent past, as an illustration of what positive and hopeful *joyous* expectation and anticipation can bless everyone with. So, Dear Ones, refrain from being caught up in negative dramas that are occurring everywhere at this time. Stay in your center of balance and focus on the feelings of joy, happiness and gratitude and you will sail through this time of purging in a blessed manner.

I wish to speak with you about finding your own niche in your every day life and existence. So many of you, it seems, look around at others who are living their mission and feel that you are not living yours to your highest potential. This makes you feel inadequate, that you not working to accomplish your mission in life, and I wish to assure you that you were each chosen to be here at this time. Just the mere fact that you are here, grounding your Light into the Earth is more than enough, Dear Ones. You do not have to be blazing in glory every moment of your day. Most Lightworkers have chosen to work quietly to bring and ground the Light, they chose to do this whilst living their normal human existence, quietly radiating their Light, quietly bringing change and healing to all those around them, their family members, their community members. Everywhere these Lightworkers go, they radiate the Light of God that never fails, and this is creating that change, for you cannot help it. You are the change that you came to be in the world and by your very presence, this is occurring.

You do not have to be blazing in glory every moment of your day.

Of course, there are many who took on greater responsibilities, for this is what it is, Dear Ones, a great responsibility, to use their gifts in a more global manner and this requires great dedication on the part of those who have chosen this avenue. It requires discipline on a daily basis, it requires dedication, constant faith and trust. It requires putting our Father/Mother, our Prime Creator, first. It requires living a life of purity, a life for the most part, of seclusion, for it is rather difficult in these days of chaotic energies to be in the world and not be of it. Most of the Lightworkers who are serving in a global manner, find that they have to limit their presence in the world and to only surround themselves with those who are open to that which they bring forth at this time.

At any moment, those of you who aspire to world service can do so by becoming more dedicated in this manner, for this avenue of service is open to all, for world service is one of the steps of Initiation in your Ascension. There are many facets of world service and as I mentioned previously, those of you who quietly do your Lightwork each day are also in world service. Everything that is given to you is a gift and this gift must be shared with all, must be shared with the world and all upon her. Carrying great gifts within one's being requires great sacrifice. It means foregoing sometimes, the attending of social functions with your families or your friends. It means arising at dawn to begin aligning yourself to your Source. It means raising your frequency level before you are able to bring forth words from the higher planes of existence. All of this is a sacrifice of your time and your effort. In the overall scheme of the Divine Plan, all of you who are upon the Earth at this time are admirably performing the task for which you came. All of you are serving in a grand manner.

For every moment that you focus on the world that you want, you are creating that very existence!

I wish to speak now about the coming days. There will continue to be 'stepped up' energy coming forth. There will continue to be great movement happening upon the Earth and within the Earth. There will continue to be revelations occurring in all facets of human life. The changes that you wish to create in the world will not happen instantly or miraculously by someone else. These are changes that you are creating, for every moment that you focus on the world that you want, you are creating that very existence. You are powerful Creators, each of you. See always the world that you want, concentrate always on that which you wish to manifest in your everyday existence rather than that which you don't want. We realize that this is a challenge, as you live in the world of duality, but that is quickly changing, for the more that you envision that which you want, the faster the world of duality is becoming something of the past. This is how great change is occurring upon your world and you are a part of that change.

More and more people are awakening and becoming open to ideas that you have known for decades. They are becoming open to the possibility that they may have existed in previous lives. They are becoming open to the possibility that there are other beings on other

61

planets in this universe. In short, they are opening to their greater potentials and are becoming more enlightened, for enlightenment means becoming aware, and this will continue until there is a Great Awakening that comes simultaneously, and from that moment on, great leaps will occur in the evolution of your planet and all upon her.

You are all in a symbiotic relationship and what affects one, affects all. There is no getting away from that!

We of the higher realms stand with you. Know that you are always surrounded by the Angelic Realms, by the Ascended Master Realms and by Cosmic Beings of Light who work with you in unison to establish Heaven on Earth, and this is, indeed, occurring, Dear Ones. Have faith. Keep working on releasing all that no longer serves you within your minds, hearts and spirit. Ask for assistance with this each day. We are only too happy to help you in this way. Keep on keeping on, Dear Ones. The world moves forward at a rapid pace now. Know that you are loved beyond measure by all of your sisters and brothers of the higher realms.

There is a continued need for Lightworkers to believe in themselves, to believe in their individual abilities and gifts. There are so many of you who are questioning at this time whether all your efforts are worth it. Let me tell you now, Dear Ones, your efforts are worth it! Very much so!

The Earth grid is lit up, a brilliant, golden white Light and every day, this grid increases its vibratory frequency and when this occurs, the Earth also raises her vibratory frequency, and so, also, does humanity. You are all in a symbiotic relationship and what affects one, affects all and what affects all, affects each one. There is no getting away from that.

The beloved Lightworkers have been working diligently for many, many years, holding the Light, anchoring the Light and centering themselves each day, becoming the transducers, bringing in the cosmic energies, and this is having a great effect, in spite of all seeming appearances to the contrary. It is, in fact, the truth. In the heart of nearly every human being upon the Earth is the great desire for a new way of being, for a new world, a world of peace, love and harmony. This great desire is occurring on a collective level, and anything that occurs on a collective mass consciousness level reverberates through the entire planetary system and great change occurs. This is what has been and is, happening at this time.

In the heart of nearly every human being upon the Earth is the great desire for a new way of being, for a new world; a world of peace, love and harmony.

Many of you are feeling challenged by the increased energy levels. Many of you have felt yourselves become transducers as you move from place to place and this is what is indeed, occurring. For instance, this Scribe and her spouse just came back from a trip to a town that was four and a half hour's drive from their home, and while there having dinner with one of their beloved relatives, she felt great energy pouring very powerfully through her feet and she was wondering what was happening, why she felt as though she was vibrating so strongly that she might just rise up and float away. What was occurring at that time was that the town that she was visiting was in great need of a Cosmic Light infusion and this was occurring through her energy system while she was visiting, chatting and having dinner in the restaurant. This is what is occurring for many of you as you go about your daily affairs and your daily business. Each of you will find yourselves being transducers in this way. Do not be alarmed when this happens, there is nothing wrong with you. It is your agreement and your willingness to be a channel and transducer for the great cosmic energies that are now streaming into the Earth at this time.

It is a great service that you are, and will be, performing in this manner, and some of you will be moved to travel when you really had no urge to do so and this will happen when it is seen that there is a great need for the downpouring of the great cosmic energies in a certain place. We work with the Lightworker who is the nearest in distance to this place and ask them and inspire them to go to that place so that this energy infusion can take place. Many of you will be called upon to do this, so be prepared, Dear Ones, it is a part of your service agreement at this time.

You are being called at this time to act as a transducer for the infusion of cosmic energies.

We see that it is a very challenging time for Lightworkers, for they are still performing their service, their disciplines, and trying to be in the world but not of it. It is a challenging position to find yourselves in but you have the abilities, you have the knowledge and you have the high frequency that is necessary in order to accomplish these tasks, so be prepared for this. When you puzzle as to why you have this urge to go to a certain area, you will remember this message and then you will connect with the fact that you are being called at this time to act as a transducer for the infusion of cosmic energies.

As we look at your world around you, we see there are and have been, many shocking events that have taken place and this will continue to occur in these changing times, as the Light and vibratory frequencies increase. Those who do not vibrate with the higher frequencies, who have chosen not to take part in the Shift to a higher dimensional plane of life, who have chosen not to go through the Ascension process, you will observe that more of these individuals will be leaving the planet and it will seem rather shocking at the amount of people that will be leaving. Do remember, Dear Ones, this is a choice that each being has made before they ever set foot on this planet.

Know that you and all of your beloved ones and their beloved ones, are always protected by we of the higher realms, the Angels, the Archangels. Each of you is dear to us and so important, for you are on the front lines at this time. You are our warriors of Light. You are the

Earth team and your presence on the Earth at this time is crucial and very, very, very important. Even though most of you are still not aware, each of you is like a blazing Sun walking the Earth and your voluntary participation in this is very much appreciated and is so crucial to the Divine Plan. Hold your Light, Dear Ones. stand in your Light. Believe in yourselves, believe in the higher purpose for which you incarnated upon this planet at this time. You are the hope of the world. You are the world changers. You are the Light beacons, the lightning rods. All is well with the Plan. All is working as planned, and even beyond the expectations of the Divine Plan.

Do not falter on your path. Do not quit, for that saying that it is always darkest before the dawn is looming on the horizon for each of you. The dawn breaks, Dear Ones. Have faith!

And so, Beloved Ones, we urge you to continue on, to keep on keeping on. Do not falter on your path. Do not quit, for that saying that it is always darkest before the dawn is looming on the horizon for each of you. The dawn breaks, Dear Ones. Have faith.

I wish to have discourse with you in regards to all the inner work that you have been doing. You have been accomplishing miracles! You have let go and released so much that no longer serves you. Continue on this path. The energies that are coming through onto the Earth at this time will not allow you otherwise, for this is the entire purpose of these great energies, the cleansing and purging energies that are occurring within every soul upon the Earth at this time. There is a Light at the end of the tunnel. Just have faith, no matter how pulled you feel into that which you are releasing from within yourselves, muster the strength to stand in your Light, to practice your daily disciplines, and it shall be released. Each time that this occurs, there is less that needs to be addressed and this is a very good thing.

On the Earth scene at this time there is much that is at work behind the scenes, through the people on Earth who are in power and also energetically, that which is unseen. There are many who are working to create great changes in the systems that have been established upon your world. There is much that is changing within these systems that will create greater equality for all upon the Earth. There are movements afoot which will establish fairness and justice for every human being upon the Earth. Know that there are many whom you do not hear about in your news media who are working to bring this about. There are many serving the Light who are not apparent at this time but will become more so as time moves on.

All the probabilities that were in effect in times past have now been surpassed and are no longer in effect.

Much has already been accomplished by the Lightworkers of the world. All the probabilities that were in effect in times past have now been surpassed and are no longer in effect. There truly is the great majority of humanity who will be ascending with the Earth when that time happens. The Divine Selves of all of humanity upon the Earth have been working together on the inner planes to bring about these changes, to ensure that every human being rises with the Earth into the higher dimensions. This has never occurred before in the history of the universe and it is of great interest to others in the Universe; for you and your Earth, are the Template, setting an example throughout the universe, throughout the Galaxy. The Earth is being observed with great intense interest and, I might add, with great joy and celebration, for the Divine Plan has surpassed itself in achieving its goals.

As ever, I ask you who read this message to test everything that you read, see and hear within your heart area, your heart chakra, for this is your connection to your Divine Self, and this is your connection to your highest truth. Always go within, whatever you may read, hear or see, always go within to seek the truth and whether what you read, see and hear resonates as the truth within you.

You are ever surrounded by legions of Light, Angels of Light. You are ever assisted. Know this and have confidence, Dear Ones.

You have been facing personal challenges, personal tests of your strength and discernment in your daily lives and this, of course, will continue, for this is the nature of the world that you are living in at this time, but I wish for you to know that all your efforts will soon be worth it. Know that the time is almost at hand where all your efforts will start bearing fruit and will start manifesting for you. You will have finished with all the work that needed to be done with releasing that which no longer served you and enter a new phase where you will be the creators. You will know that which you invoke will manifest, you will know the great responsibility that you carry as a representative of the Light of God that never fails. You will know this, Beloved Ones. Each of you has been tested and tried, each of you has understood your responsibility. Each of you has taken greater steps to achieve your personal Mastership of Life upon this plane, knowing and understanding the power that you carry through your thoughts and intentions and that is a great accomplishment, Dear Ones!

Trust in the process that is occurring, trust that all is in Divine order, trust in yourselves, in your inner guidance and in the guidance from those of us from the higher planes who work with you. All is always according to the highest good for all concerned. All is always done in accordance with the highest good of all in each of your personal lives, and upon the world scene. Continue on being the beacons of Light that you are, continue in your releasing process. Soon you shall emerge cleansed and purified, into the next step, the next phase of your work upon planet Earth, at this time in her history.

I wish to bring to your attention a very important fact...of the need to take action each day in order to be the Co-Creators on this Earth. You are the human instruments of the Divine and as such, it requires action and dedication on your part. This requires a daily space of time to bring the cosmic Light into your own auric field and into the core of the Earth. It requires expanding your own field each day, for your auric field expands more than you know. Your auric field covers thousands of miles when you are in your highest vibratory frequency.

You are the human instruments of the Divine and as such, it requires action and dedication on your part.

When you meditate, when you decree or repeat your affirmations or prayers each day, your auric field extends, and what I am suggesting for you to do as soon as you complete the raising of your vibratory frequency fields, is to state your intent that this frequency field be held in place until the next day, so you can build upon it...so that you never lose the frequency level that you have established the day before, and so on and so on. This will create a great deal of stored power within you and you will not have to struggle to regain any that has been lost through being human upon this Earth. Always you will have that reservoir as a starting place as you go about your day. All that is required is the daily adherence to your disciplines, for that stored energy does no one any good if it is not used.

The cosmic energies continue to stream into the Earth and anchoring into the Earth through each of you. You are serving admirably in your chosen and voluntary service. There are more and more of your Lights lighting up the world; more spheres and globes of Light that are coming forth that were not lit before, and of course, that means that the rest of humanity is Awakening, and it is so exciting for we of the higher realms to see. When we see this, we rush to the side of the newly Awakened

One, and Angels are assigned to each one and we work with them from that moment forward. There are legions of Angels ready to serve, that surround the world. All one has to do is call upon them, all one has to do is intend and ask for them to come to your assistance and to give you guidance on a daily basis, and this is then, so.

Wherever you go, you are impacting every human being who comes into contact with you!

Many of you are dedicating each day to the Light of God that never fails, and this creates great joy. As you do this, and as you give gratitude in humbleness for the gifts that you are receiving and for the remembrance of your task in the Divine Plan, and you work your Plan each day, this Light grows exponentially. You may not know this, but when you go out into the world, into your shopping malls, into your banks, into the stores, in your work places – wherever you go, you are impacting every human being who comes into contact with you. This is of great importance. This is one of your functions, in your tasks upon the Earth, and as you go out, the Violet Flame that surrounds each of you ignites the auric fields of those you come in contact with and they begin to remember their reason for being here on Earth at this time. This creates what you might call 'spontaneous combustion'. This Light is beginning to spread in your communities, in your cities, in your nations and across the entire world. You are more powerful than you realize, Dear Ones.

Never be afraid to stand in your Light - the days of hiding your Light are over. The time is *now* to shine forth, the time is *now* to be the Light that you truly are in every facet of your life. You came to ground this great cosmic Light into your every day, mundane existence that it may become a part of humanity and the mass consciousness and this is now happening at an accelerated rate. There is a great impetus of this cosmic Light moving across the Earth, not only *into* the Earth but *across* the Earth. As this is occurring, more that was hidden is coming to the surface until there shall come a time when all that has been deliberately withheld from the people of Earth will no longer be able to hide behind any corner, and this truth WILL come forth. Believe this, Dear Ones, and never falter in your task, in your disciplines. This is what we are all working towards.

There shall come a time when all that has been deliberately withheld from the people of Earth will no longer be able to be hidden and this truth will come forth.

We see so many Lightseekers. Do you remember that phrase, Dear Ones, this is how each of you started out, you were Lightseekers and now you are Lightworkers, and even beyond that, you are Emissaries of Light upon the Earth. Be gracious, patient and kind to the Lightseekers, and know that each of them is already a great Being of Light who is in the process of the discovery of the Light that they truly are. Extend a helping hand when you are asked, but remember the great rule, and that is, you must be asked, just as we must be asked by you, you also upon the Earth who are Emissaries of Light, must be asked before you can give assistance. You are living on a free will planet and every being upon the Earth has sovereign rights and free will.

As your perceptions grow and expand, you will see much in the Lightseekers that they do not yet see, and so we caution you, Dear Ones, to always ask for and get permission from them before you can come forth with information and give assistance in this way. Each being has the sovereign right to make their own choices and decisions, each being has the right to go at their own pace, and each being has the right to set their boundaries. It behooves each Lightworker to honor those boundaries within self and others. So in your desire to be of service, remember this. Remember that each human being on the Earth has boundaries that one must not overstep. If you see a way that can help someone, you must first ask if they give you permission to give them further information. This is the way of the higher realms, this is the natural Law.

More of you will be called into service to become transducers, to give of your Light to others. More of you are now coming into your talents and abilities and it will become clear to you how you may serve further. We stand with you, we applaud each and every one of you and we love you dearly.

- Chapter 5 -
Change Requires Your Effort

I would like to discuss with you the great strides that you have been making in your own spiritual progress. Not only are you raising your frequency level, you are also gaining great insights into issues in your own life, into issues with others, into issues with the world in general and into the concerns that you have. Truly, you have gained so much, and as you continue in your disciplines each day and you repeat your decrees, your Light continues to grow and expand in frequency and vibration and you advance higher as you gain more insight and perspective and this is how spiritual growth occurs.

Altogether, there are many thousands of you around the world, who are standing in your Light, who are decreeing for a better world, who are decreeing for peace, love and harmony upon this planet, and your efforts are starting to bear fruit. Keep on keeping on! As you continue to do this, your Light is igniting the Light in others and as this is occurring, there is more Light being generated and radiated across the Earth. This is how the Light spreads, this is how the Earth is changed for the better.

Intend that your frequency level be doubled each day when you repeat your decrees. I have a further suggestion and that is, at the end of your decreeing each day, intend to hold and anchor this energy within your body and your chakra system so that it is available for you to use next time and by doing this way you will never lose the gains that you have been making but will continue to build on them. This is of great importance.

People all over the world are creating great changes by decreeing Light, affirming Light, visualizing Light in whatever modality of work that they use. As more of you are doing this, it is creating powerful transformation upon the Earth. Know this and be heartened, for you are doing an excellent job in igniting the Earth and humanity into a higher space. More and more of those people who did not 'get it' are 'getting it' now. They are beginning to understand the importance of giving of their energies in this way each day, they are beginning to understand that this is how we change the world, that it does not happen by waiting for 'others' to come in and save this world. Rather, it is done through your own efforts, and this is what is happening and what you are accomplishing. Well done!

Change does not happen by waiting for 'others' to come in and save this world. Rather, it is done through your own efforts.

This time is a most propitious one in the history of the Earth. This time has so many golden opportunities that are being presented to each and every one of you, including those of you who are reading this information for the first time. Do not forget to intend and ask each day that all the energy downloads that are available from all God sanctioned sources of the greatest Light and the highest truth be downloaded to you. In this way, you will leap forward in your spiritual progress; you will leap forward in remembering who and what you are, in becoming the co-creators that you truly are.

We see many of you as you repeat your decrees or do your meditations, affirmations or visualizations; we see more of you perceiving yourselves as great TALL beings of Light. This is excellent, this is who and what you really are and it is very helpful to continue to visualize and see yourselves in this way. This adds empowerment to you and it adds even greater power to that which you are decreeing and affirming, visualizing or meditating upon. Know that you who want to volunteer to be transducers of higher energy must state your willingness and intent each day. Each morning, state that you are willing to be transducers for the cosmic light energies and then you will be put into action many, many times. This is having a positive effect as more beams of Light are streaming forth from the Earth into the cosmos. As this occurs, the Earth becomes more of that which she is destined to be, a beautiful shining Star! This is her destiny and it is the destiny of all humanity who choose to transform with her. This is what is occurring at this time with all downloads of energy that are available from all God sanctioned sources that are entering the Earth's atmosphere for your ultimate highest good.

Your bodies are transforming and changing, you are becoming crystalline beings.

Your bodies are transforming and changing, you are becoming crystalline beings and the crystalline energy is running like a river in the marrow of your bones. You are pulsing with the high frequency energies that you have been assimilating, integrating and downloading and this in turn, is creating a new humanity, for you are becoming super human. You are just at the edge, at the very cusp, of beginning the manifestation of the superhuman beings with all their gifts and abilities that you are bringing as gifts to the world. More of this is coming to Light into your conscious daily acknowledgement and use. Do not forget to call upon these energies that you have been absorbing and integrating. As you do this each day, your power grows exponentially.

You are catalysts who are activating your sisters and brothers around you to seek the Light, to tread the lighted pathway. Those of you who are in this space of co-creation with Prime Creator and the Ascended Host are the ones who will be leading the way. The ones who will be guiding your sisters and brothers, who will be lending a helping hand, who will be offering courses and knowledge that will assist them. They will gain much from what you offer them by having already done

74

the work, by walking your walk and talking your talk. Having stood in your Light and persevered, you have made it so much easier for your sisters and brothers to get onboard. They will pick up the concepts of spiritually based living much more quickly in the personal ways required of them. This is what you have been accomplishing every day as you continue along your path.

When feeling overwhelmed, take a walk in nature!

We of the higher Realms rejoice when we see you, you have come so far in such a little space of time, and that is the power of people united and focused with the same vision, this is the power of the people and you are that power, Beloved Ones. Do continue to stand in your Light! The great download of energies that continues to take place is now working their way through you. You have been feeling these energies and it has translated into intermittent pain that travels through various parts of your bodies, it has translated into requiring greater rest and sleep. It has required you to nurture yourselves and take good care of yourselves.

These are powerful energies that are streaming upon the Earth and it is important that you get the rest that you need. It is also very important that you drink at least eight glasses of water every day, this is absolutely necessary to help you integrate these energies. What is required at this time is to nurture, be good and kind to ones self. When feeling overwhelmed, take a walk in nature, soak in a tub of water with some sea salt or Epsom salt in it, try to relax, listen to high vibratory music that uplifts your spirit, listen to the sounds of the birds chirping outside your window, listen to the sounds of nature and ask your own divine essence to fully integrate one hundred percent of the energies that you are receiving each day so that this takes place with grace and ease.

This energy continues to purge and cleanse and those who have not been preparing for the downloads of these energies are experiencing them in more uncomfortable ways and since they are not aware of what is happening, they do not understand what is occurring within them and this is creating fear and panic in some of your sisters and brothers. We ask you, Dear Ones, to continue each day to ground the Light into the Earth, for it is crucial at this time. Through your individual efforts it is you who keeps stability within and upon the Earth.

It is important to focus your energies in unity with others to create the Heaven on Earth that we all desire.

Each Lightworker who chose to come to Earth at this time is an integral part of the Divine Plan to create peace on Earth, to create harmony, to create a new civilization, a new way of living upon the Earth. They came to find a way to restore the Earth and bring all of her inhabitants into a life that is a Heaven on Earth. This has started to occur now, but it is not an easy experience, so be aware of this and send your sisters and brothers your love and your healing energies and thoughts.

It is important for you to be in total control of your thought processes at this time. Keep your thoughts ever on what it is you truly want and do not be sidetracked by those who would create debates, for these serve no purpose, especially at this time. All they do is pull your energies away from that which is important. Learn to be discerning about this, Dear Ones. It is fine to give your opinions, but know that endless debate is just a waste of everyone's energy. It is important to focus your energies in unity with others to create the Heaven on Earth that we all desire so that humanity can step into the Golden Age.

It is wondrous to see the power that you generate when you utter your decrees, when you sit and meditate, when you visualize the world that you want. This concentrated and united effort is creating daily miracles. These are not easily discernable upon the Earth's vibratory frequencies yet but shall become more so as time continues. All of a sudden, there will be reached a point where humanity as a whole clicks in and 'gets it'. That is the day that we are all working for, Beloved Ones.

76

Do not falter in your efforts; pray, decree, meditate, visualize, create the world that you desire with all of your heart and soul. Give of yourselves each day to make this so and let no one sway you from this. Let no one else's doubts create doubt and fear within you. For you know within your heart and soul that you are on the path, the path of Light, that is the path that you chose. Others may have chosen another way, so do not doubt yourselves but continue creating more Light each day. As you do this, your own spiritual awareness grows as knowledge, insight and remembrance will come back to you. You will remember that you are a powerful being of Light in the days ahead

Love has the power to heal, love has the power to transmute; love has the power to create miracles!

The time of choosing has come upon the Earth. On the inner planes, the Great I AM Presence, the divine essence of each soul incarnated upon Earth has made the choice to rise with the Earth into her Ascension. Of course, there are those who have chosen not to go through the Ascension with the rest of the Earth and all upon her for various reasons and purposes, with some choosing to be on this side of the veil to help out and to give of their great energies here. Be assured, Beloved Ones, that each soul, whether incarnated on the Earth, or whether beyond the veil, is intensely working with all their might to bring an awakened awareness to every human being upon the planet. It is the desire of Father/Mother God, it is the desire of Mother Earth, that all join with her and ascend into the higher vibration.

Your Light is creating greater Light upon the Earth. Each time one of you repeats your prayers, decrees and affirmations, or meditates or visualizes, there is greater Light upon the Earth and within the Earth, and this is most wondrous to behold. Please remember, Dear Ones, that the greatest force in the Universe is LOVE. Love has the power to heal, love has the power to transmute, love has the power to create miracles. It is the most potent power to create change in this Universe. We ask you to open yourselves to receive more love within your hearts, we ask you to *feel*, each day, *feel* with your heart, whatever challenge, lesson or situation is in front of you; *feel with your heart* and know that the first initial feeling that you have is your higher guidance speaking to you. Learn to listen to that first initial feeling and it will never steer you wrong, for this is your highest guidance.

You who have been preparing yourselves as transducers of higher energies must be able to transmute this energy into the Earth.

As more group meditations continue to occur across the Earth, with their group focuses, know that this also creates more impetus for the greater forces of the great cosmic energies to stream upon the Earth, so you who have been preparing yourselves as transducers of higher energies must be able to transmute this energy into the Earth and then allow the Earth to flow the energy back through you and out into the cosmos. This helps to distribute the energies in a safe and protected manner so that your sisters and brothers upon the Earth have an easier time of it. Your great love and compassion in volunteering for this effort is very commendable, for those are the qualities that an Ascended Master must embody before they can become a Master of Life upon a physical planet.

I want to bring to your attention the impact the new energies are making upon your four body system – the physical (or fleshly body), the etheric (or energy body), the emotional (or astral body) and the mind (or mental body). Each of these bodies interpenetrates each other. As the downloads come in, these new energies upgrade your DNA, and what occurs then is the cleansing and purging, not just of your physical body but your etheric, emotional and mental body. This process goes deeper and deeper within and as your body system refines, more Light is created and anchored within you. Your connection to your divine essence becomes stronger and the communication between you becomes much clearer. This will continue until your divine essence can fully integrate with your four body system, which is the reason and purpose for these downloads. It is a gift from the Creator to help humanity prepare for entry into the higher dimensions.

You are becoming your divine essence!

It is vitally important to ensure that you follow your inner guidance in these times to listen and act upon your inner promptings. Your divine essence is working diligently to establish a permanent connection that is strong and unbreakable. You are becoming your divine essence and as this connection continues to build, there are more subtle bodies that begin to be built as you progress along the spiritual path. Thus the need to listen to your inner guidance; your divine essence will know what is required in each moment for optimum integration. You may be guided to drink more or perhaps less, water. You may suddenly find yourself at a page on the internet that advertises a nutritional supplement, you begin desiring a certain food, or you may be drawn to a certain healing modality or feel a sudden desire for a thorough back massage...all of these are coming from your inner guidance which knows the best way to help the integration process proceed with grace and ease. Your task is to become more attuned to this guidance and follow it promptly. This requires the elements of faith and trust to act upon what you are given.

Your divine essence is working for your ultimate highest good and it behooves you to be willing to go with the promptings that are given. Know that this is the refinement that is now taking place within the Lightworkers who have been practicing their spiritual disciplines regularly. This process will continue and your multi-dimensional awareness will awaken progressively as your body of Light continues to grow. There will be a moment when this integration takes place and then your way will become much clearer and easily discernable. There is always upward and forward movement, when one level is reached; the next higher level opens to you and so on. With all the new energies coming in each day, filled with codes of activation, you need to be consciously aware of what is occurring and not lose heart. As has been said before, 'The only way out is within.' You must spend the necessary time to truly know yourself, for that is where freedom lies.

You must spend the necessary time to truly know yourself, for that is where freedom lies.

When you know yourself, you are connected to an ever stronger flow of energy, consciousness and awareness and your way is more certain and filled with Light. You begin to walk lightly upon the Earth; you no longer create or participate in human dramas, or waste your energies in the endless programs that can pull you back into duality consciousness again. One example of this would be the area of politics, another is religion. These two areas of human existence have kept the human spirit floundering on the lower levels of consciousness and awareness for eons, the first, through endless debates and concepts of separation and the other, through control and manipulation of a negative manner, for example, the disempowering concepts of guilt, sin, wrongdoing, etc. It is time for you to become aware of these programs that have been so well established upon your planet. You are now in the process of recognizing and releasing attachment to these. Once this is recognized for what it is and that it limits you from embracing your endless possibilities, intend that it is cleared from you and replaced with the cosmic Christ Light.

It is especially important for Lightworkers everywhere to stay centered and calm. Envision the world you would want your children and grandchildren and future generations to live upon, a world of peace and harmony, joy and abundance, prosperity for all, limitless possibilities that are open to all. Be steadfast and unfaltering in your daily disciplines and intend and see yourself as the empowered human/spiritual being that you truly are. See that you are the agents of change; that by your persistent intention and effort, your vision for a new and peaceful world will manifest. Send loving, healing thoughts to the central core of Mother Earth and all the kingdoms upon her. Call down and through you, the fuschia pink love light from Venus and visualize and feel it anchored into the crystalline core of the Earth. See this beautiful wave of color permeating everyone and everything upon the Earth. Intend love, BE love, create love, Dearest Ones.

You are the agents of change; by your persistent intention and effort, your vision for a new and peaceful world will manifest.

I would like to focus upon the full integration of all the energy downloads that you have been accepting into your beings during all the great cosmic events that have been taking place in conjunction with the Earth. These energies are of the highest frequency and what will be occurring is that you will be facing all that which does not vibrate with this highest frequency. What is now beginning to come to the surface from within you and others into your daily lives is what you need to recognize and understand as old energy and take note that this is what is occurring so that you do not become a part of that old energy, that you merely observe what is taking place and recognize it for what it is. Send it forth for transmutation into the great cosmic Christ Light.

There have been great events occurring in the etheric realms that are not discernable to you at this time. Great feats have been accomplished. Mother Earth is firmly on her path of Ascension and all of humanity upon the Earth is once again given the opportunity to make the choice to ascend into a higher consciousness.

As you go about your daily lives, you will be meeting with people who have just been awakened. Many who come into your field of resonance will be expressing that which is not of the highest frequency level so I am suggesting that you remember to place your protective shields around you, to affirm and decree your daily protection. I ask you to also add in your decrees, that this great shield of protection of the great cosmic Light be wrapped and surrounded around each of your loved ones and their loved ones. This is very important, Dear Ones. You are like lightning rods and all that is being released for transmutation at this time immediately heads for the nearest Light, and in many cases, you are IT, so know this and always surround yourselves with your protective shields so it will not affect you on the physical, emotional, mental and spiritual levels. This is to make you immune to these negative energies that are being released for transmutation.

Continue to wield your Light each day for the healing of your beloved planet.

It greatly pleases and heartens us to see the number of people who are now on board and online in working with the Family of Light. As we continue to work together in this way, great strides are being made in the upliftment of the energies of the Earth, all her grids, all of humanity and the Kingdoms upon her. This is amazing and wonderful for us to participate in, knowing that we are now working together as a team, as a union of the greatest forces that exist within the Universe. For it is now 'as above, so below', as we work together for the highest good of the Earth and all upon the Earth. This is wondrous in itself and a never ending source of awe, thankfulness and gratitude from those on this side of the veil.

You are becoming more proficient in your daily disciplines. Those who decree use this discipline with greater knowledge, knowing that you are the Creators. Every time you repeat your decrees, you understand inherently that you are the Creator manifesting upon this Earth. What you are manifesting, Beloved Ones, is miraculous. Continue to wield your Light each day for the healing of your beloved planet, for the upliftment of Earth and all upon Her.

Humanity is now seeking the Light, they are becoming aware that there is something in the air, that there is something greater that they should be looking for and this is a very positive development. You will notice in the days ahead that this is becoming very noticeable, where those who once mocked you and scoffed at your beliefs, now come to you for clarification, for greater understanding and now you begin your role of teacher on a global scale by becoming teachers and living examples within your own communities.

Ensure that your hearts are pure, that you are egoless in your desire to serve others.

You are the light beacons and you will be sought for that reason as more of humanity begins to recognize that there are greater and higher forces at work in this world and the universe. You and your abilities will be sought more often. Each of you has your own plan, your own mission and each of you will bring forward that which is a blessing to this world and to these masses of people who will be seeking that which you offer them. Those of you who are healers, artists, channelers, writers, researchers, you and your work will become more recognized and sought after. Be prepared, Dear Ones, to become truly multi-dimensional beings manifesting upon this world. Your talents, your abilities and your Light will be sought by those who have just awakened.

Ensure that your hearts are pure, that you are egoless in your desire to serve others. This is very important, for you bear a great responsibility to those who come to you seeking the Light, seeking greater knowledge, that you impart this to them in the greatest purity and clarity as coming from the Light of God that never fails. As you do this, greater prosperity will just automatically flow to you and through you. All aspects of your daily existence upon the planet Earth will be harmoniously supplied, and your storefronts and your work will be sought after.

If you have not yet begun your life's work, we advise you now to daily go within and connect within your divine essence within your heart space and you will be guided to do that which is your greatest joy and pleasure. This is your life work, for gone are the days of self sacrifice, gone are the days of suffering, gone are the days of putting others' highest good above your own as you now offer your individual gifts to the world. In serving in this way, with your greatest joy and pleasure, you meet the needs of all and most importantly, your self, in order to manifest as the great being of Light that you truly are. The integration with your divine essence is continuing each day, you will recognize this process by quite gracefully and with ease, releasing all that no longer vibrates at your new level of frequency. That which seemed so difficult to do before, now becomes so very easy to do.

You will be guided to do that which is your greatest joy and pleasure. This is your life work.

You will realize and understand that you walk in a mantle of Golden Christ Light, that you are blessed beyond measure; that you are your Christed Self walking the Earth. You will be filled with wonder that this has come about in such a joyous and wonderful manner. This is your freedom; this is the freedom flame fully manifest upon the Earth. You, in your sovereignty are now walking the Earth fully discerning, fully functioning as the Light bearers that you are.

We of the higher realms absolutely adore you and we bow to you for the great work that you have been doing on behalf of the Earth and all of humanity, on behalf of the Divine Plan for the Earth all the while honoring your own parts of the Divine Plan and your divine essence. Well done, Beloved Ones, well done!

I want to address the various messages coming through that talk about 'chaos' energies and the interpretations of these energies that are coming forth. Dear Ones, all energies that flow throughout the Universe can be considered 'chaos' energies and one would need to examine these energies on a personal level to understand what that means. All new energies never before experienced can be called by this name, as experiencing them can lead to transformation and change, and isn't this what you are all working towards? As transformation of the consciousness of humanity occurs it can be viewed as 'chaos' and yet, the ultimate result is a greater consciousness that all of humanity can then work from.

You are becoming a multi-dimensional human, able to traverse many different levels of consciousness in a single instant.

You are becoming a multi-dimensional human, able to traverse many different levels of consciousness in a single instant. You are remembering that you are part of the Infinite One and that there never was a separation. This will soon be occurring for many of you. The energy downloads have created a movement forward in your evolution, although it is not readily apparent at the moment. As you are integrating these downloads, remember the basics - plenty of water, rest, time in nature, nurturance of self, quiet time for reflection and connection with your divine essence. As you go within, you will always be 'in the flow' of the current happenings and you will see that you are always guided on your path.

We of the higher realms have been speaking to you of the need to feel and express joy and gratitude during these times because these feelings are higher frequencies that can keep you connected to the Source and also keep you in a sovereign state of being. These frequency levels can keep you lifted in your highest vision. When you express gratitude, it sends these energies out into the Universe and more blessings begin to occur to keep you in this state, so that you always have more to express gratitude for. Joy is your natural state of being for you are all beings expressing as the Creator expressing as itself in the innocence of expression, in exploration of its Creation. Staying connected in this way helps you to integrate the new energies with more ease and grace and prevents you from falling back to that which you have left behind.

Know that you are supported by many beings of Light as you walk your path each day. You are never alone. Love truly is the most powerful force in all the Universe. As you stand in your Light each day, you are a carrier of this Light and you automatically heal people and situations by your presence. Sometimes, this healing comes in the form of the release of negativity in those around you and you must understand the reason for it, Dear Ones, and be patient. Change is not easy for many on Earth today and it will come through the power of love. You will begin to see and experience this in your daily lives very soon. Many changes are transpiring within each soul incarnated upon the Earth and each soul here at this time has made the choice to go through these changes.

The impetus for change will grow ever greater until there shall come the Great Awakening.

Be patient with others and most of all, with yourselves, your day of remembrance is soon upon you. What a day that will be in your experience, Beloved Ones! Truly, you have worked hard to bring this to pass and it shall be added unto you. As you wake up each morning in your daily lives, know that you are creating your new world by your thoughts, words, deeds and actions. You are changing the world in this way, and as more of you come online, the impetus for change will grow ever greater until there shall come the Great Awakening.

I wish to speak to you about the new energies and how they are affecting the Lightworkers and humanity in general. The Lightworkers, who have been working for many years, in many cases, decades, in developing their Light quotient, are at this time absorbing great amounts of the wondrous frequencies and energies. As you do so, because you are taking in so much more than the average person, you find that there are periods of adjustment required at times. If you are persistently asking for these downloads each day, you are more than likely finding yourselves experiencing pain in various parts of the body, and especially along your spine. This is not dangerous but can leave you feeling lethargic and feeling that you are not moving forward at all. As you are accepting and assimilating these energies, there is discomfort, but know that these are the times and the opportunities to avail yourselves of that which is freely given. You will feel great gratitude for these infusions in the times ahead.

As you wake up each morning in your daily lives, know that you are creating your new world by your thoughts, words, deeds and actions.

Humanity as a whole is reacting in a different manner. There is a bombardment of unresolved issues coming up from the depths of their beings that some term 'the shadow self'. This is the part of each person which has been programmed to think unvoiced thoughts of criticism of self and others, of doubts they have about their self worth, some find their criticisms and judgments of others welling up within them which keeps cycling through them until a final resolution, such as understanding, comprehension and forgiveness of self and/or others is reached. Many are running to the medical practitioners because of all the unusual symptoms they are experiencing, such as severe bouts of dizziness, headaches, nausea and a host of other complaints. This is the great cleansing, Dear Ones, of all that will not stand the Greater Light of the higher dimensions that you are all swiftly moving into. There is no escape from it, all must go through 'purgatory' and you are all in it together. Love yourselves and all others. This too, shall pass!

- Chapter 6 -
The Process of Transformation

The Earth has moved into a different 'space' and is now in the cleansing stage also. Truly, this is a symbiotic relationship, and your love for the Earth and all upon Her is most appreciated. It is a time to 'go with the flow' and just allow what is in each moment without the old paradigm programs of 'shoulds' and 'musts' holding you back. What you are all going through is of such cosmic proportion that it is mind boggling for most of you to wrap your mind and comprehension around. We advise you to do what your body, mind, heart and spirit feels like doing in each moment, within reason, of course, as most of you still have to function in your daily work and straddle both worlds simultaneously.

What you are all going through is of such cosmic proportion that it is mind boggling for most of you to wrap your mind and comprehension around.

We are amazed at your tenacity and courage and hold you in the highest esteem and we are including your awakening sisters and brothers in this also, for they also chose to come here on Earth at this time. All of you considered it an honor and a privilege to be chosen to actually take part in this process. And this process will continue, Beloved Ones. Humanity as a whole is being accorded the opportunity and benediction of Prime Creator to awaken to their chosen roles in this momentous cosmic cycling. The love and compassion of those who are aware and awake is most needed now.

It is love, the greatest power and force in Creation that is the 'glue' that binds all together.

Try to see the entire picture and understand that it is love, the greatest power and force in Creation that is the 'glue' that binds all together, and it is Love that is your greatest ability to give. You are the bridge builders, Dear Ones, you have come to walk the middle way and effect change with every move, thought, word and deed that you make. We see more and more of you coming together and uniting in a common cause, realizing that even something as simple as signing a petition that brings awareness to others and which is delivered to your government representatives is an act of great importance. This is how you reclaim your individual sovereignty. As more of you come together in this way, you are creating the changes you desire, for when your government representatives see the mass of people who want change, they are affected by this and are comprehending that the old ways of doing business will no longer work.

I would like to discuss with you how you may begin to move forward in the new energies that are inundating all upon the planet at this time. There are greater ways of working with these, and involves listening and perceiving the clues and advice that we give you within channeled messages, and it requires that you compile these suggestions into a powerful invocation for yourselves and repeat this on a daily basis.

Now this is a great clue that I am giving you this day! There are wonderful suggestions for catapulting yourselves into higher frequency levels that come through the various human channels that we all work with and it requires that you compile and save those snippets of positive affirmations or invocations that are indicated. Save these and compile all into a Master Invocation for yourselves. This requires you to become diligent in reading every message that comes forth. Each message will contain a clue or information that is advice or a suggestion for you, the reader, to embrace.

Then, take that part of the message and save it to a new file and as you continue on in your reading you will come upon more statements of power, save those also. Before you know it, you will have created for yourself a powerful invocation that will, upon repeating this on a daily basis, set you on a quantum leap forward in your spiritual journey. It requires the discernment of being able to pick out that which will serve you by repeating it each day. This is what this Scribe does. She keeps compiling statements to herself and as she progresses in her frequency level, she discovers more and more of them, and uses that as a means of lifting herself higher and higher. As you practice this, it will become easier to do, and you will recognize instantly those words that help you to your highest and greatest good in the next stage of your journey.

You are magnificent Beings of Light and illumination!

So we suggest to you, Beloved Ones, open your minds to all possibilities, search each message. Wherever you may land on an internet search, search that, knowing that you were sent there for a reason, that in the information that you were lead to, you may come to the next step on your journey that will help catapult you into the higher dimensional levels of consciousness. That is the 'Name of the Game' now, Dear Ones. Catapulting yourself into all possibilities, for truly, that is where you are headed now. Truly these great opportunities are open to you and will continue to be so.

I say to you, search with the intent of finding the wording that will serve your higher vision and intentions. Take everything that you wish to embody in your new life, write it down into a Master document, and then work on it to personalize it for yourselves. You are the Masters, do remember this, Dear Ones, you are the Creators of your lives. Live, dare to live, the Life Magnificent! You are magnificent Beings of Light and illumination. Each moment that passes upon the Earth plane, each moment that you stand in your Light, your multi-dimensional Light bodies are glowing with radiant, scintillating Light, sparkles of Light, magical Light.

It is a great achievement to transcend all the seeming limitations of living in the physical world but still be in the world.

There is great movement afoot. Each and every day, there are more inroads being made by all the Lightworkers on the Earth, so many of you are now gathering together in groups. It is wonderful to behold the amounts of people who are gathering together, who are intending to gather together to honor this glorious new start into a new way of being and doing upon the Earth.

Many of you come to this website to read our messages because they hearten you, they fill you with hope, they fill you with inspiration, they fill you and empower you with our Light and our love, and that is the true purpose of this portal, this website. It is to hearten and unite Lightworkers around the world, that they will have a place where they can come to focus in a unified effort, to see what is required in each given time of the movement in the world. As we all work together in this way, wonderful accomplishments are being achieved and that has delighted and surprised even we of the higher Light realms. We are completely delighted with the willingness of the Lightworkers of the world to band together in common purpose. It is so wondrous to behold.

We are coming upon a time, Dear Ones, that will open up unlimited possibilities for you and that is why I have given you the hints and the clues, for it is time to step beyond your seeming limitations and take on your unlimited possibilities, your unlimited potentials, for that is where you stand. You have done your work, Beloved Ones, you have added your Light and you continue to do this each day and you are now ready in your frequency levels for the next step. To step into unlimited potential and explore this within yourselves and your daily lives. This is also part of your task, to bring the great Beings of Light and your unlimited potential manifesting upon the Earth as the pattern makers, as the way showers for the masses that are even now awakening to their own possibilities and potentials. All are now able to see such wonderful alternatives to that which they have been entrapped to believe for most of their lifetime.

Stretch your minds, go beyond, use your great imagination and create yourselves anew!

Many of you will become shining examples of the greatness of the human spirit, for it is a great achievement to become a Master of Life on the physical. It is a great achievement to transcend all the seeming limitations of living in the physical world but still be in the world. This is what you are, and have been, doing for your entire lifetime. All is coming to a completion, and this completion means that you have overcome all the pitfalls of manifesting in a physical world such as the Earth has been and are recreating yourselves to become unlimited Beings.

We of the higher realms are filled with excitement to see how you are becoming very creative in what you ask for. This is a wonderful development and we are filled with joy to give you assistance in every way that we can. Know this, Beloved Ones, continue on, don't feel that you are being too demanding, know that you must reach even higher into your unlimited potentials, for this is how wonderful and new changes are, and will be, created. It is by you surpassing your previous perceptions of yourselves and demanding even greater things. This is how life in the Golden Age begins. We are always available at your beck and call, Beloved Ones, it is our greatest joy to serve you.

I wish to speak to you about the continued need to become more aware of that which is coming up for your review. As the new energies continue to flood the Earth, it is important that you watch the emotions, thoughts, feelings, old mental and emotional programs and insecurities that come up, that well up from within you. For these as they come up need to be acknowledged as something that needs to be observed and released. If you can do this and intend that it be transmuted and released forever from you, it shall be so.

It is very important for you to set down, in writing, all that you intend and desire for yourself, for the world and state it with great intention each day.

The important thing, Dear Ones, is to not get caught up in these old energies, thoughts and programs again, but to recognize them for what they are – old energy – and release them forever from you. As you do this, the thoughts that begin to come up from within you are those that you were not even aware that you were holding within yourselves. Release these and replace with something more positive, with an intention for a new you, for your new life of unlimitedness; for all that you have ever dreamt about and were always prevented from becoming. You can become everything that you dream about, Beloved Ones, it requires dedication, it requires awareness, it requires intention, it requires determined effort, but you can create the world and the life that you personally desire. It is now up to you to be the Creators, it is up to you to understand this and realize the responsibility and the great joy and adventure that this can become in your lives.

Stretch your minds, go beyond, use your great imagination and create yourselves anew! In the new energies, you are stepping forth into the New Earth and creating as you go along. Ensure that your thoughts are of the highest intention and integrity, ensure that your aspirations are those that bring you joy and happiness, that contribute to great positivity in the new consciousness of the Earth and all upon Her and, it shall be so.

We from the Ascended realms and the Angelic realms, are waiting to be called upon and are eager to be of service. We delight in working jointly with you in creating, not only changes upon the Earth Herself, and in raising the vibration of all upon the Earth, but also, working with you to bring to fruition your aspirations, your dreams and desires, for a better life, for a better way. We stand ready to assist. We are able to do this, so even if one thousand of you call upon us at the same time, we are able to be with each of you at the same time, because we, and you, are multi-dimensional Beings, and it *is* possible, because all things are possible. It is our joy to be of service, it is our joy to be called upon. Every day, ask for what you want, nay, demand what you want. Be bold, be creative, be fearless in stating your intentions for the highest good of all.

Rest when you need to, take breaks when you need to, experience joy, gratitude and happiness, find pleasure in simple things, walk in nature, play in nature, laugh!

You are now entering your personal mastership, and you are fine tuning all that you have learnt, all your perspectives, readjusting and realigning; just as the Earth is realigning to Galactic Center, so you are aligning. In every facet of your lives, all is being realigned to the higher purpose and your higher intention and that is why it is very important for you to set down, in writing, all that you intend and desire for yourself, your families, for the world and to state it with great intention each day, that it may become manifest. Always be aware that what you ask for will come to you so be entirely sure of what it is that you truly want, and work on the clarity and intent of your wording so that it is always for your highest good and for the highest good of all concerned.

Many of you are beginning to envision yourselves as larger than your Earth, as larger than your Universe and mentally stepping outside those boundaries and looking back. This is a very good exercise to place yourself in the new paradigm, to place yourself as the unlimited being that you truly are. It is important to see yourselves in this way, for this is how you help anchor unlimited potential into yourselves and the Earth and this exercise in turn, helps to uplift all upon the Earth, for it is you, the Beloved Lightworkers who are daily increasing in numbers, who are accomplishing this miracle and it is a miracle, a wonder to behold. We see your Light shining from the Earth and unite with the energies that are being sent from the highest realms of Light and Galactic Center. This combined Light helps to light up everyone and everything upon the planet. You are all interconnected and when one person shines their Light brilliantly and fearlessly, it enables and empowers their neighbor or their friend or associate to do the same.

You have heard for so long that the change is upon you now and so you wait for the now to happen. Well, Dear Ones, the now is happening!

Speak your truth, join and support all endeavors that have as their purpose bringing peace to the world and creating joyful change upon it. Your efforts bring in gratitude and thanksgiving, harmony and understanding amongst all the people of the world. These are all ways that are emerging now that you can support by joining, by signing up, by stating your intention that this is the ideal that you support. This in itself creates a movement of Light and love, peace and harmony upon the Earth.

You have been busy integrating the new energies and learning when to move and when to rest and lay low in order to assimilate the new energies and you are all doing great. We see you feeling overwhelmed at times and your bodies feel tired, but that you are honoring this when it happens. You are learning that it is always advisable to rest when you need to, to take breaks when you need to, to experience joy, gratitude and happiness, to find pleasure in simple things, to walk in nature, to play in nature, to laugh. These are all positive ways to bring the highest potentials into your life, into your selves. Yes, there will be challenges, for you are like vortexes of Light and all that is not of the Light seeks you but you have the ability now to create your own world. You know that all you must do is recognize the challenge before you, do what you can and then release and detach yourself from it and it will not be an energy that 'sticks' to you for resolution later.

Never cease to focus upon the highest vision that you desire for yourselves, your loved ones, all of humanity and the Earth.

You are all becoming Masters of your own lives and it is exciting to see this. Continue to work upon yourselves, ferreting out every old issue and thought as they come up and transmuting and releasing them. At this time that is all that is required as you assimilate the new energies in the greatest ease, comfort and safety that is possible. By having this as your intent each day you will continue to shine your brilliant Lights, Beloved Ones.

I wish to speak with you about preparing yourselves for the great influx of energies that is now pouring down upon the Earth from the highest Light realms. The frequency of these energies is extremely high and you must continue doing your utmost to ensure that you accept and allow this energy to enfold you and permeate all aspects of your being and your life. Continue to do this, Dear Ones, for this is of great importance in your own spiritual progression.

This is the new way of being, as you and all upon the Earth move upward in frequency and vibration. This process needs to be accomplished in the quickest possible time in order to move into a higher space, in order that those who have plans and who do not have the best interest of humanity or the Earth in their intent will not have a chance to implement their plans fully. Now, you inherently know all of this and that is why you continue on in your work, that is why you continue to bring in and anchor the Light every day. We thank you, Dear Ones, we thank you for your dedication and the purity of your purpose.

We thank you for diligently maintaining your daily disciplines and we realize that it is a difficult challenge for you, as it seems that the more you rise in the frequency levels, the more you have to clear. You are being continually faced with clearing the old energies from your entire Being, and also being the representative of the higher energies by being the bridge between Heaven and Earth. This is very challenging for you at this time, but we say to you, Beloved Ones, it is well worth it! Know this, and continue on keeping on.

The whole of humanity wishes to live in a world of peace and harmony, where there is enough for all, where everyone has all of life's basic requirements.

You have heard for so long that the change is upon you now and so you wait for the now to happen. Well, Dear Ones, the now is happening. Stay in the now moments in your lives, this is what will stand you in good stead in the days ahead, for by staying in the now and being alert and aware of all that comes before you for your awareness, for your processing, for your discernment, is that which will serve your highest and greatest good. We, as the whole of the Ascended Light Realms, are endeavoring to clear the greatest of the densities from the Earth in the quickest possible time, so that is why you are experiencing an acceleration of your ascension symptoms. Whereas before we tried to make it as comfortable as was possible while working on you, we are now moving ahead in quantum leaps, and in some instances, your physical body will be striving to catch up, to raise itself into the highest frequency levels along with all the other multi-dimensional bodies that you truly are. Your physical body has been adapting admirably to this great influx of the new crystalline energy.

Your bodies are transforming into crystalline Light. Soon your consciousness will start remembering, it will allow you to visit timelines of your past as well as timelines of your future, and paradoxically, you can do this while being in the now moment, in full consciousness, clarity and awareness. There are those out there in your world who are proclaiming cataclysms, Earth movements and changes and we say to you again, Dear Ones, that all that has been prophesized has been surpassed exceedingly up to this point and that what occurs from this moment on to the Earth and all of humanity is subject to the will of each one of you. You are the creators and you are creating your new world as you go forth in each now moment. Know this and never cease to focus upon the highest vision that you desire for yourselves and your loved ones, all of humanity and the Earth, for this is what you are creating, and indeed, have already created, as we are fast approaching the time when the new world will manifest and come forth.

Do not try to move ahead of the capabilities of your physical, denser bodies, for you require your physical bodies in order to continue with your mission!

Know that your Earth is transforming, just as you are, and that you are in a symbiotic relationship, as I have said several times before in other messages. Become more aware of the energies and the sounds and the vibrations that are coming to you from the Earth through your feet, through your auditory channels. This Scribe hears the Earth's hum, which is a low, thrumming sound, that she had a hard time adjusting to in the beginning, but now it is a part of her everyday life and she is becoming synchronized with this and this will help her in the times that are just ahead of you.

We say to you do not be discouraged, for humanity itself as a whole, has responded to the Light. The whole of humanity wishes to live in a world of peace and harmony, where there is enough for all, where everyone has all of life's basic requirements.

The Earth recognizes all who work with her, you who anchor the cosmic Light into her crystalline core every day, or as often as you are able, for there is no rule set in stone about this, all is voluntary. The

Earth acknowledges and honors each of you for the service that you are rendering to her, to all of humanity and to all the kingdoms upon her.

We thank you for all of the efforts that you are so earnestly performing. Most of you are not aware of the great good that you are contributing at this time in the Earth's history, but that time is coming, Dear Ones, when each of you will know the great good that you gave. You will be honored for your efforts, you will be acknowledged for all the Light that you have anchored into the Earth.

You are now synchronizing the inner with the outer!

I'd like to bring to your attention so that you will know when you have been infused with more than your accepted daily quotient of the higher vibratory frequencies. This will show up in your life as sleepiness and the need to rest your physical bodies, to drink more water, to become passive and nurture yourself in various ways which were discussed before. Remember that, if you are decreeing and you feel the energies swirling around you or through your spine, through your feet, through your crown chakra and your heart chakra, know that usually means that it is time to stop for this day. Honor this within yourselves, Dear Ones. Do not try to move ahead of the capabilities of your physical, denser bodies, for you require your physical bodies to continue with your mission.

Life is continuing along a path of no return, life is speeding along on the Earthship called Earth into a greater Light, a greater future. Greater possibilities exist around you. You have but to ask, you have but to conceive and it is done. Do not be afraid to voice your intentions, for whatever Earthly desires or goals that you wish to accomplish, this is the time to set the bar, this is the time to go beyond, this is the time to create miracles, use this time. You can do this by creating a joyous, playful attitude and decreeing, invoking and affirming that which you want without feeling self conscious about it. Realize that you have been heard whether your thoughts are voiced or not throughout your entire lifetime, so this is nothing new, you are now synchronizing the inner with the outer, and by voicing this through your voice, you are setting those waves in motion to the universe and the universe responds to the same degree as the intention, clarity and focus that you have sent out with your thoughts and intentions.

Continue each day to raise your frequency levels as high as you can safely go.

Continue to practice this, Dear Ones, although the forms on the Earth are changing, there will still be a need to meet your daily requirements, there will still be a need to draw to you financial resources in the form of money. That will not disappear from the Earth in a drastic manner. It will be a gradual affair, so do practice your invocations and the voicing of your intentions for that which you want to create in your life and make it so.

We ask you to see yourselves standing around the planet Earth, expanding yourselves into huge beings of Light and love. Hold your hands out to the Earth and send forth your love into the Earth, into her crystalline core, into all the grids of the Earth, assisting in the activation of the great crystals that are now ready to come online. Take a few moments to do this during your other activities and see yourselves as greatly expanded beings of Light for that is truly who you are. We know that those of you who have the capability of doing this can greatly add to the energies and intentions for the moments of this time. Know that we from the ascended Light realms, the Galactic realms and the Cosmic realms, are all adding and magnifying your energies, for this is how we work together in unison.

I wish to discuss with you the concept of working within the new energies that are pouring down upon the Earth at this time. These are very powerful energies and some of you have been and will be feeling a little nauseous at times as this energy continues to permeate every cell and atom of your physical, mental, emotional and spiritual being, and as this occurs, there is a slight feeling of nausea that occurs. This is a continuous ongoing process and as it continues, the feeling of nausea will leave. You might also be finding yourselves having moments of dizzy spells. This, too, shall pass, Dear Ones. Continue each day to raise your frequency levels as high as you can safely go. It is very important to do this at this time, not only for your own comfort, but also to help in raising the vibratory level of the mass consciousness of humanity upon the Earth.

Be assured, Beloved Ones, the masses of humanity are on the brink of awakening!

It is the great focus that we are working upon, for as we cleanse and transmute the mass consciousness of humanity and dissolve the crystallized negative thought forms of fear and lack and every other negative, limiting quality that has kept each human being in bondage for thousands and thousands of years, we from the Family of Light are asking for your assistance. Call down the violet flame of transmutation each day, repeat it as many times as you have time for, in your cycles of seven, or eleven, or even, thirty-three. It is of inestimable value at this time.

Send your love to this crystallized mass consciousness grid, directing all your energies into transmuting this with love, Light and compassion, for humanity at this time who have not yet awakened are in the throes of facing their greatest fears, worries, doubts and it is looking to them as though the world has gone mad. Those of you who have been disciplining yourselves, who are the Lightworkers, you have gone through your disciplines, transmuted most of this out of your systems now, it is just a matter of 'fine tuning', as it is termed.

Now is the time that you can add greatly to transforming your Earth on a daily basis. The changes that are occurring are happening so much quicker than ever before. Every day there are many changes that are occurring within you and within the Earth and in her atmosphere. In every part of Earth, there are changes that are occurring, and all the kingdoms of the Earth are all working together in unison. We are all working to transform your beautiful planet into the great being of Light that she truly is.

Humanity must be released from this controlling grid of mass consciousness; humanity must break through into the Light, into a different way of viewing things around them. As this is accomplished, the walls of illusion around each human being are being dissolved, the walls of glamour will be seen for what it is and mass awakenings are beginning to occur. Be assured, Beloved Ones, the masses of humanity are on the brink of awakening.

You have noticed the greater infusion of the new energy within your systems. Your heart feels as though it is expanding, as though you are filled with helium or air. This feeling comes and goes, and I wish to inform you that this feeling that you are experiencing is your divine self, integrating more fully with you into your heart center, into your physical body and is surrounding you. As this process continues to occur each day, you will notice that you are being guided unmistakably by this divine presence within your heart.

You will notice when you are in contact with someone of a lesser vibratory frequency or with someone who does not wish you well that you will feel this instantly within your heart. There will be a pain and you will know that this means that the energies or the person that you are in contact with is not the best energy to surround yourselves with.

On the positive side of this infusion of new energy, you will notice as you practice your daily disciplines of prayer, decreeing or meditation that this feeling of lightness within your heart grows and expands. This energy can be helped to grow in power by visualizing a great sphere of golden white Light within your heart chakra growing and expanding, pulsing and sparkling with pure crystalline golden white Light. This is of immense benefit and has an exponential positive effect if you can manage to do this for a few moments each day.

We also notice since the infusion of these higher energies, that there are many people who are approaching you with their issues, with their negativities. These are people who have not awakened, these are those who have not yet learned to take full responsibility for themselves; for their thoughts, actions, words and deeds; and indeed, some have yet to realize that they are the creators of the circumstances of their lives. They feel as though they are victims, and that someone else is always to blame. It is advisable at this time, Beloved Ones, to send these individuals your greatest love and absent yourselves from them.

Have compassion, Dear Ones, but know that it is a no win situation for you, for these individuals have not yet comprehended their own power at the most basic levels. If you try to give them assistance, all that you will do is become mired in their dramas and their issues and thereby lose the momentum that you have gained so dearly by your daily practices.

Even though we say that you are becoming One and that we are all One, at this particular moment in the Earth's history you must protect yourselves, for you are still not in a place of detachment from the sufferings of others and therefore, you can quite easily fall prey and become enmeshed in their dramas and issues very quickly and this is why I bring this to your attention.

Find that which gives you pleasure and enjoyment and do those things. Laugh each day, Beloved Ones, look at the world with humor, look at yourselves with humor, for are you not wondrous beings? Each individual is so unique, here to give their greatest talents, skills and abilities to the world. The new world awaits you.

- Chapter 7 -

You Are a Force for Change

I wish to speak to you about the continued need to become more aware of that which is coming up for your review. As the new energies continue to flood the Earth, it is important that you become aware of and begin to watch the emotions, thoughts, feelings, old programs, and insecurities that well up from within you, for these as they come up need to be observed, acknowledged and released. If you can do this and intend that it be transmuted and released forever from you, it shall be so.

The important thing, Dear Ones, is to not get caught up in these old energies, thoughts and programs again, but to recognize them for what they are – old energy – and release them forever from you. As you release the thoughts that come up from within you, you are realizing that they are things that you were not even aware that you were holding within yourselves. Release these and replace them with something more positive, with an intention for a new you, for a new life of unlimited potential. You can become everything that you dream about, Beloved Ones. It requires your dedication, awareness, and strong intention, it is true, but you can create the world and the life that you personally desire. It is up to you to be the creator, to understand this and realize the responsibility and the great joy and adventure that this new way of living can become in your lives.

Stretch your minds, go beyond, use your great imagination and create yourselves anew! In the new energies, you are stepping into the new Earth and creating as you go along. Ensure that your thoughts are of the highest intention and integrity; that your aspirations are those that bring you joy and happiness. Ensure that they contribute to the enhancement of the new consciousness of the world, and it shall be so. Every day, ask for what you want, nay, *demand* what you want. Be bold, be fearless and creative in stating your intentions for the highest good of all.

Ensure that your thoughts are of the highest intention and integrity; that your aspirations are those that bring you joy and happiness.

We from the ascended and angelic realms are waiting to be called upon. We are eager to be of service, to work jointly with you in creating not only changes upon the Earth herself, and raising the vibration of all upon the Earth, but also, working with you to bring to fruition your aspirations, your dreams and desires for a better life, and a better way. We stand ready to assist. We are able to do this even if one thousand of you call upon us at the same time, we are able to be with each of you at the same time, because we, and you, are multi-dimensional beings, and it is possible, because all things are possible. Do ask us, for it is our joy to be of service, to be called upon.

You are now entering your personal mastership, and you are fine tuning all that you have learnt; readjusting and realigning all to your new perspectives. Just as the Earth is realigning to Galactic Center, so are you also aligning.

Every facet of your life is being realigned to the higher purpose and intention for it. That is why it is very important for you to set down, in writing, all that you intend and desire for yourself, your families and for the world and state it with great intention each day, that it may become manifest. Always be aware that what you ask will come to you, so be entirely sure it is what you truly want. Work on your wording so that it is clear, for your highest good and for the highest good of all concerned.

You are beginning to envision yourselves as larger than your Earth, as larger than your universe and mentally stepping outside those boundaries and then looking back. This is a very good exercise for placing yourselves in the new paradigm as the unlimited being that you truly are. It is important to see yourselves in this way, for this is how you help anchor unlimited potential into yourselves and the Earth. In turn, it helps to uplift all of humanity and everyone and everything upon the Earth, for it is you, who is accomplishing this miracle and it is a miracle, a wonder to behold, to see the beams of Light that you are emitting coming from the Earth. The higher octaves of Light and energies being sent from the highest realms of Light and from Galactic Center, and also from the different planets and galaxies helps to en-lighten everyone and everything upon the world. You are all interconnected and when one person shines their Light brilliantly and fearlessly by being it, it enables and empowers their neighbor, their friend or their associate to do the same.

Speak your truth with love in your hearts, join and support all endeavors that have as their purpose the bringing of peace and the creation of joyful change upon the world.

Speak your truth with love in your hearts, join and support all endeavors that have as their purpose the bringing of peace and the creation of joyful change upon the world. Bring in gratitude and thanksgiving by being it; bring in harmony and understanding amongst all the people of the world. These are all ways that are coming into being now and you can support them by joining these activities or by stating your intention that this is the idea that you support. This in itself creates a movement of Light, love, peace and harmony upon the Earth.

You have been busy integrating the new energies and learning when to be active and when to rest and lay low in order to assimilate them, and you are all doing great. We see you feeling overwhelmed at times and your bodies feeling tired, we also see that you are honoring this awareness when it happens. You are learning that it is always advisable to rest when you need to, to take breaks when you need to, to experience joy, gratitude and happiness, to find pleasure in simple things, to walk and play in nature, to laugh. These are all positive ways to bring the highest potentials into your life, into your selves. Yes, there will be challenges, for you are like vortexes of Light and all that is not of the Light seeks you for transmutation, but you have the ability now to create your own world. You know that all you must do is recognize the challenge, do what you can and then release and detach yourself from it so that it will not be an energy that 'sticks' to you for resolution later.

When you have fully embodied your Divine Self, the Earth will change dramatically!

You are all becoming masters of your own lives and it is so exciting to see this. Continue to work upon yourselves, ferreting out every old issue and thought as they come, acknowledging, transmuting and releasing them. At this time this is all that is required, that you transmute and assimilate the ongoing transformation in the greatest ease, comfort and safety possible, having this as your intent each day. Continue to shine your brilliant Lights, Beloved Ones.

I wish to touch upon the fact that you have now stepped into the new dimension and that it is just a matter of transmuting and releasing the last of the old tendencies still embedded within your being that you may not even be aware of. All limiting thoughts and beliefs need to be observed, acknowledged, cleared, transmuted and released. This is an ongoing process that will continue to occur in the years to come, but many of you are well on your way to clearing your entire body system in preparation for integration with your Divine self.

There is great joy and celebration in the ascended Light realms that this accomplishment is being implemented. When you have fully embodied your Divine Self, the Earth will change dramatically, for you will be walking the Earth as a representative of the Christ Consciousness. This is something that is not given to many, it is something that is earned and it is also something that you already had before you came here. It was a conscious permission on your part to forget all that you truly are when you came to the Earth plane, in order that you may truly know what it is to live in the lower densities, so that when this opportunity came in this auspicious time in the history of the Earth, you would be well versed in the ways of the Earth as an Earth human and you have done that extremely well, and have truly forgotten your great glorious presence.

You are transforming into the unlimited beings that you truly are.

This is now in the process of being changed, in the process of transformation. You are transforming into the unlimited beings that you truly are. As this happens and you anchor your Divine Self within you, the more the vibration on the Earth automatically undergoes a change. If you are worrying that you do not know what your mission is, or where you should be or what you should be doing, we say to you that it is not necessary, just continue to work upon yourselves, continue to raise your frequency levels, continue to cleanse and release all that does not resonate with that higher vision of integration with your Divine Self. As this continues and as more Light comes into your physical self, more of your Light body becomes activated.

The Earth and all upon her will change. The vibration and the frequency level upon this planet will rise to a higher level and all of humanity, in turn, will rise along with that vibratory level. This is why you, the Lightworkers, are so important. You are the ones who are changing the world by staying true to your disciplines and beliefs, by honoring yourselves, and by raising your vibratory frequency levels. You bless the Earth and all upon her as you do this and this has been a gradual process. As more of you cleanse, clear and release, absorb and integrate more of your Light bodies so too does the Earth and all upon her. All are helped, for everything that happens upon the Earth is in accordance with your visions, your decrees, your thoughts, words and deeds each day. It behooves each of you to remember this and act responsibly with all of your thoughts, feelings and emotions. Yes, you are clearing and cleansing and when it is time to cleanse, you will release verbally, mentally and even physically that which needs to be released. Do not dwell upon this, acknowledge that you have now released it and that was the whole purpose of what has come forth, to acknowledge it and release it and move forward, ever gaining in frequency and vibration.

This is the Great Work at this time – to cleanse, transmute and heal.

The Light upon the Earth is growing in clarity and intensity. More work of transmutation is continuing to occur. This is the Great Work at this time – to cleanse, transmute and heal. The Earth and all upon her are enfolded in the cosmic energies, frequencies and Light. The violet transmuting Flame is in action continuously, as is the emerald green healing ray. There is a golden Christ Light that surrounds all. There are Galactic energies that are being beamed upon the Earth as gifts for those who are willing to receive these gifts. I am making you aware, that if you desire to receive gifts of knowledge, art forms, music and abilities, new technology, new ideas, then, Dear Ones, ask each day and let it be known that it is your intention to receive these gifts and they shall be added unto you.

Your bodies are transforming. Your entire being is being changed from within. It is important to realize this and honor yourselves, honor your feelings, and be in touch with your bodies. If your body says rest, then rest. If your body and your mind desire to be out in nature, then honor that. Get out in nature, and partake of the Earth's vibrations. The time now, Dear Ones, is to transmute, cleanse, release, receive, integrate and assimilate, so do continue on with this task. Do continue to be patient with yourselves and each other, and to understand that this is a process that the Earth and all upon the Earth are going through.

Along with you, each being upon the Earth is going through it at their level of understanding, at their own level of frequency, and all are being affected by these energies, all are being transformed. All is as it should be; all is continuing to take place in a great positive expansion. Keep your minds ever focused upon your goals, do not become distracted or turned from your path by that which would set you in fear, and take you off your path. It is your sense of calm and centeredness, it is your anchoring the Light into the Earth that is keeping the Earth in stability, and keeping the energies balanced that are leaping about at this time from humanity. It is your stabilizing energies that are making a difference.

Start your morning in gratitude and fill your days with thoughts of joy and the appreciation of the beauty that is around you!

Understand that each soul is choosing the way that they shall go, whether they consciously understand this or not. Send each being around you your love and Light, breathe and remain calm. Start your morning in gratitude and fill your days with thoughts of joy and the appreciation of the beauty that is around you; the beauty of nature, the beauty of the Earth, the beauty of the souls that surround you each day in your circle of love. Be thankful, and know that beyond the Earth, we of the higher realms surround you with our love and our Light and we wait for you, beloved people of Earth, to call upon us, much more than you do currently. We are ready, able and willing to be of assistance, not only in your personal lives but in being called into action to help in Earth situations, to help in cleansing the Earth. We are here to assist, call upon us!

I would like to have discourse with you about what is happening in your daily lives, your personal lives, in your countries, and the happenings in the world. There is much that is changing on a daily basis, there is much information that is being revealed across the internet, information that sounds credible, and information that has the ring of truth. I tell you now, Beloved Ones, there is much coming forth that is not of the highest truth and it behooves you to go within and connect to your own Divine self within your heart space, and there you will know the truth of a thing. If you read, see or hear something that has a ring of truth, give it this test, the test of going within and listening to your heart. This is the time of much illusion, the time of all energies flowing and spiraling around you; the time to walk with care and caution, and to call upon your guidance, both within and from those of the Light who surround you. Know that you are guided and protected, and also that it is your task to stay grounded and connected to your Divine selves. Call upon us whenever you need to, we are here for you.

You will always be guided to do the right thing for *you* at the right time.

On a daily basis in your daily lives, life will continue as it has for many years, most of the changes are being made on the etheric levels at this time. Most of the changes are behind the scenes and are energetic in nature. You will be always be guided to do the right thing for you at the right time. As we have said before, you are situated in the areas where you are needed most. This will become clear to you in the passage of time.

Many of you have wondered why you keep staying in an area when people are unfriendly or treat you as though you are invisible. It is because, Dear Ones, to the people around you who are not yet awakened, you are invisible to a certain extent. You are vibrating at different levels than the people around you and when you talk about what is happening in the world around you, they literally cannot compute what you are saying and actually blank you out. This can be very disconcerting and frustrating to you, if you are unaware of what is happening. This is why I am addressing this now, so that you can become aware and be prepared.

There will eventually come a point of connection, but at this moment in your time, this is what you will be dealing with more frequently. Try to stay in your heart center at all times and let your love and compassion flow from you. If people around you don't seem to hear you, let it be, just send them love! Everything continues to unfold as it should, the people of Earth are awakening and this will become more evident in the next few years. Many of you have been worrying about your loved ones who are still not awakened and what will become of them. Know that there will be many events taking place that will inspire each being upon the Earth to awaken to the truth of who and what they really are. This is not necessarily going to happen through drastic changes and events.

You are the unsung heroes of this time.

The beloved Lightworkers of the world have been steadily growing in numbers and the Light that has been generated by them continues to affect the mass consciousness field which has been cleansed of much dross and continues in this process each day. This is why your daily disciplines are so important. We need the Earth team members on task. Remember that we are all working together to raise the frequency levels of the Earth and all upon her. We continue to do this. You are the unsung heroes of this time. You all work unceasingly for love of your Creator, the Earth and your sisters and brothers. You inherently know the need for it. It is the reason you are here at this time.

Continue to stay on your spiritual path, and walk ever in the Light of God that never fails. You are ever the shining beacons of Light walking the Earth and your efforts are much appreciated. You are the bridges between Heaven and Earth and even though this is a difficult task, you are well qualified to succeed. Many of you have done this before so that you know what to do. Your greatest challenge at this time is to find yourselves unfocused and distracted by the world around you. It is the new energies ever increasing in intensity that creates this anomaly within you. If this has been happening for you, then you must find the will to become more disciplined in focusing on your task to raise your Light quotient, for as you do this, so too, do you raise the Light quotient of every man, woman and child upon the Earth.

From the higher realms, we see more of the whole picture and you are doing far more good than you can ever know in your present circumstances. Keep on keeping on, Beloved Ones.

There is a great cleansing occurring and there are many who have pretended to be of the Light who now find themselves being exposed for who they really are. These are the agents that could be termed 'double agents'. We ask you, beloved Lightworkers, to become very discerning about whom you give your energy and attention to. It is by their works that you shall know those who are not who they present themselves as, even to the extent of offering advanced services to the Lightworkers in terms of initiations and activations.

Your body is your Temple, a sacred vessel that houses your Divine self and is the instrument that manifests this Presence upon this world!

Those who are offering their services to truly help other Lightworkers and the awakening ones have a high energy emanating from them, and this is a palpable energy even when you visit their websites. This is the energy of a highest vibration which is love. You will instantly feel this love within your heart chakra and know that you are in the presence of one of the transformed ones. One who walked through the spiritual fires of trial, test and tribulation and emerged shining and purified, having overcome all of their temptations, tests and initiations. These were set up many ages ago as a way to ensure that only those of the purest intention and character could have access to the more arcane knowledge that required these attributes. You who are reading this definitely have been steadfastly walking this path of Light.

The important initiations occur on the inner planes and most of you do not remember the ceremonies that you partook in. Walking the path of Light requires absolute integrity, honesty with self and others, the upholding of one's honor and the clarity and discernment of truth.

These initiations become progressively more refined as you continue successfully on your path of Light. Those who are high Initiates know that great self discipline and restraint is involved. It requires opening oneself up to unwavering scrutiny of self, to purify all aspects of duality and lower vibratory thoughts, feelings, actions and deeds. It requires letting go of the eating of flesh in most cases, it requires taking on a more purified diet of fresh, natural grown foods such as fruit and vegetables, drinking pure, clean water and the practice of breathing techniques.

When the respect for all of Creation is honored, the Earth will indeed be a better place.

These requirements have been somewhat modified because there are so many of you now incarnated upon the Earth. Many of you still consume foods that have no life force energy in them at all which includes most of today's packaged products. Anything that is not fresh from the vine has already lost a great deal of its life force. We see many more of you in future years understanding the need to expect high life force energy in every food that you consume. This will be changing the way that food is prepared for your consumption. The desire for processed foods of no food value will fall away and as a consequence of this, the health of all individuals will be improved tremendously.

Do try to become aware of what you ingest into your bodies, for your body is your Temple, a sacred vessel that houses your Divine self and is the instrument that manifests this presence upon this world. As you cleanse and purify your physical bodies, the world around you becomes more pristine and healthy. We see that when enough of humanity chooses to stop the eating of meat, the air will be cleaner and the energies in the Earth's atmosphere will be lighter. When the respect for all of Creation is honored, the Earth will indeed be a better place. As the body Temples are kept purified, so too, the emotions of joy, happiness and equilibrium become the norm for each soul who walks the Earth. So you can see, Beloved Ones, there is still much work to be done.

The work that we are doing together is the way of the peaceful warrior. We work with energy and effect positive changes in this way!

Those of you who heed these words will find the Ascension process much easier to deal with, for there will be less dross taking away your higher energy in order to keep your physical bodies in a balanced state. A truly healthy body is a joy to manifest in. A truly healthy body permits all the highest vibrations to flow through unencumbered in any way and so there will be great and inspiring creations such as books, poetry, art, sculpture, in many modalities that will be created and come from humanity. They will joyfully express their talents and abilities as their contribution of energy exchange. The enjoyment of these creations by one's fellows will be the energy exchange that they give in return. Can you fathom such a world? That is what will eventually transpire for you. All of your efforts at this time will be worth it, Dear Ones.

Try to imagine such a world and spend some time each day visualizing a world where everyone is doing that which gives them joy and happiness every day, a world where one does not have to rush off in heavy traffic to work for eight hours and then slowly find their way home again through heavy traffic, in order to make payments on a house and property that you cannot even enjoy because of being too busy in the striving for it to truly do what you love. This will change, Dear Ones, there will be a different way, a better way, and it is you who is creating this now.

I want to talk to you about the increase in the intensity of the cosmic energies that are pouring down at this time. These energies are opening up the pineal gland which is the next step in the ascension process. Many of you are already starting to feel pain in the pineal gland area. This will continue to increase each day so that this process does not cause extreme pain for anyone. Most of you should be able to get through this process without too much discomfort. However, we do advise that you continue to practice your daily disciplines in order to match the rising vibratory frequencies.

This is a most exciting time, not only for the Earth and all her inhabitants, but also for the entire universe!

Many of you will also be hearing sounds within your inner hearing. This is also part of the pineal gland opening and you will soon be able to hear and recognize the frequency sound (signature) of your Guides, etheric Teachers, and the Angelic realm as they come near you. Each has a signature that is unique to them, just as you do. Soon there will not be any way that you can hide your self from those who can discern energy signatures. This Scribe is able to discern energy signatures from certain people even when their names are not attached to email messages which come through other people. She always senses the true signature behind it and discerns who it is really. This is a very wonderful ability to have and this ability is opening within many of you now. On the higher levels, this is the norm. We are all known by our energy signatures. So as this ability becomes noticeable for you, begin to practice listening for our energy signatures. We are all around you during your daily activities no matter where you are.

There have been many Angelic guides assigned to you and if there is a need for more, they are instantly at your side. You, the mighty Lightworkers, are our front line warriors of the Light. The work that we are doing together is the way of the peaceful warrior. We work with energy and effect positive changes in this way, and I want to say that you are doing wonderfully well in this. Most of you have energy flowing through you on a constant basis and your energy meridians have been growing larger and more opened, so that the increased frequencies are able to come through you without discomfort to you.

You have been experiencing increased feelings of joy and well being. This is excellent for keeping your energy and frequency levels high and this will continue to develop each day and soon this will be the natural state of being for you. You will always walk your spiritual path with calmness and equilibrium. There is a growing sense of excitement in the air and an anticipation of something wonderful happening soon. We feel this from our stations too. Much will be taking place both on the etheric levels and upon the Earth. Change is the natural order of things now. The momentum of the increased Light cannot be stopped so be prepared to walk around in a state of bliss and joy!

You will discover that relating to others becomes a joyful experience, as a new sense of love fills each heart upon the planet.

Know that all is coming together to a point of stillness, what is referred to as zero point. This is a new territory for all and so we watch and see the probabilities and possibilities unfolding. This is a most exciting time, not only for the Earth and all her inhabitants, but also for the entire universe. Every star nation has members observing and ready to assist us at any time. As we have told you before, you are all considered heroes, for it took great courage to come down to the lower dimensions and agree to forget your Divine origin. Soon remembrance will be upon you. The Light upon the Earth that each human being radiates will light up the entire world and everything will be changed to the positive. There will no longer be any place left for darkness to hide. All will be exposed to the Light and the truth.

We stand with you, Beloveds, we are but a breath away. Know this and carry this knowing in your golden hearts at all times. We are all one.

I want to address the need for you to diligently pursue the processes of purification in your bodies, minds and deeds. I know that this is a tall order at this most challenging time but the need to stay in your integrity has never been greater, and the more that you can do so, the more grace and ease you will experience in your purging processes, and at the same time remain true to your commitment to 'walk your talk'. Those around you are awakening and asking questions that may strike you as invasive, for most of you have more or less isolated yourselves from others, in order to maintain your high levels of frequency, which is not easy to do in the company of others who have not the same intention or awareness. The time of isolating yourselves is coming to an end and you will discover that relating to others becomes a joyful experience, as a new sense of love fills each heart upon the planet.

Your bodies are continuing in their transformation and the transformation stops for no one now, including those who are not awakened yet.

Imagine if you will, walking down the street where everyone sees you and takes the time to smile and greet you. No matter what shop you enter, people smile and have time to pay attention to you and fulfill your needs. This is what is coming down the pathway for you in your not too distant future. There will be a greater desire to serve each other without expecting anything in return. Each will be acknowledged and honored for their contribution; for you will recognize that each soul has something of immense value to give for the enjoyment and empowerment of others. Those who receive will understand that a part of that person's own energy is imbued in the offering and will honor this. Gone will be the days of competition and striving for recognition. Each person will be honored for who they are; a beautiful, shining and loving soul, here to shine and pursue that which gives them joy.

This is the time to nurture yourselves as many of you have been releasing so much that has been stored within for so many lifetimes. It is the time of cleansing, clearing, healing, balancing and integrating. Being good to yourselves and taking the time to acknowledge your body Temple and giving thanks for its loyal and unending service to you all these years is a good thing, Dear Ones. Your bodies are continuing in their transformation and the transformation stops for no one now, including those who are not awakened yet. Many are finding their way to their doctor's office with symptoms that cannot be explained and therefore are unalleviated. Many are also succumbing to the fear presented by those in power at this time about epidemics that are not in actuality developing. Much awareness about these has been spread far and wide across the planet and people are beginning to question the validity or value of taking the suggested solution. The world is waking up!

Those on the path of Light continue as best they can to stand in their Light and truth while at the same time, cleansing, purging and transforming within their body Temples, all the while maintaining their personal integrity. Know that you have help - just ask - most of you have become so ingrained in walking your lonely path throughout these years that you fail to ask. We can help in a myriad of ways and we know that you deserve, so please do not feel that you are being selfish or asking too much. It is our greatest joy to be of service to you, Beloved Ones!

Continue to prepare for any eventuality and be open to the signposts that are occurring even now. Much will come forth that will create a great release on the collective level of so much fear that it will change the world for the positive in a very short space of time. On the higher dimensions, we are in celebration for that which is to come. Stay true now to your disciplines and to your selves, for you are becoming one unified being of Light. Speak to your Divine selves out loud and let them know that you know they are real. Start a line of communication and you will find the connection growing stronger in each moment. The descension is now occurring rapidly and there shall come a time of the meeting and integration of higher and lower aspects, a most joyous one! Prepare yourselves, Beloved Ones.

– Chapter 8 –
Know Yourselves

I want to talk about the need to stay centered within self. There is a lot of information that is coming forth at this time that is creating a feeling of hopeful expectation amongst the awakened ones of the world. Know that your high state of expectation is creating a most positive effect upon the energies being played out upon the Earth. Every time one of you raises your frequency level as you do your daily disciplines in the feelings of joy that you are experiencing, it creates matching energy that goes out into your world and it is helping to awaken the people around you. There are more people now who are taking back their own power and sovereignty, who are questioning all that they hear or read. In order to do this, they must connect within themselves and as they do this, more Light is turned on within them! This is a very positive and exciting turn of events from our perspective.

Many people who would not even give a thought to the events that are occurring around them before and did not question what they were told on the news media, are now feeling incredulous that they have been listening to stories that are not in fact, true. People are becoming impatient with the coverage of the news that is being presented and are becoming more discerning and seeing the patterns of why and how these stories are presented. When they see their neighbor or relative forwarding emails to them questioning the necessity of being vaccinated for an illness that is not nearly as epidemic as touted by the media and even sending links to the so called 'conspiracy' websites, then Dear Ones, you know that a great awakening is occurring all around you.

You it is who have walked that path before them. Each of you went through a period of seeing past the illusions that were and still are, being constantly bombarded upon the world. You discovered a different story, a different perspective that made you feel very uncomfortable at first, as you began to realize that there has been so much happening in the world that is an entirely different scenario from what you had been able to perceive before.

You are overcoming all that needs changing in this world through the power and intent of love.

And you went through a process of denial at first, but finally you saw the new perspective as having some validity and you became adept at seeing this at work in the world around you to the point where you then had a choice...did you choose to lose yourself in the new thoughts and revelations and walk upon that path, valiantly fighting against what you had discovered, or did you wisely understand that it is through a totally different way that the Light of understanding must be brought to the Earth and all her people? I think you know the answer to that question, for here you are at the forefront of humanity, blazing trails of Light, of love, of goodness. You are overcoming all that needs changing in this world through the power and intent of love, of strong will to bring the Creator back into your lives. In this way, you have done the greatest of service to humanity as well.

Many of you cannot even watch a movie without cringing at the violence and grossness depicted. You have moved so far into the higher frequencies that it is difficult to partake or participate in these 'entertainments', for you see and understand that at their core, these 'entertainments' are really 'entrainments' that are conditioning you and your sisters and brothers to believe in a world that lacks goodness, decency, and integrity. You are making a choice to stay in the higher frequencies by not partaking of these. In this way, Dear Ones, you have been standing in your Light and grounding it into the Earth and creating the template of a better way, a better world, where humanity is in touch with the goodness that they truly are within their hearts and souls. By making this choice, you are creating powerful energies for change and are awakening those around you by not accepting what is presented to you as the absolute truth, for you know the truth and it is setting you free and your sisters and brothers as well. You are powerful Creators and you are creating with love in a peaceful way through the choices that you make.

You have discovered the joy and simplicity that comes to you by always honoring your Divine self.

This is how profound changes are occurring in your everyday world. By the choices you make each day, in each moment, knowing that your choice must always be in honor of the Divine spark within you. You have discovered the joy and simplicity that comes to you by always honoring your Divine self. In reality, there is nothing complex about being the Light that you truly are and always have been; all that is required is *KNOWING YOURSELF*. When one knows one's self, there is no room for confusion or doubt. You simply do what must be done, and we see this in each of you. Each day, you know that you must align with the Light in order to fortify you throughout your day as you go about the business of living in the world you have left behind in your consciousness. What is happening now, Beloved Ones, is that you are no longer walking a lonely path; for now your sisters and brothers are starting upon their own paths of awakening awareness. The torch you have carried for lifetimes is beginning to grow ever brighter now. Know that you are not alone. You have a myriad of comrades walking with you and you have but to call upon them and they will be at your side in answer to your call.

I want to speak with you about connecting with your Divine selves. Now this is something that has been happening more frequently to more of you. How do you know that you are connecting with your Divine self? Most often, the outer self becomes more loving and compassionate, more inclined to focus only upon that which is for your highest good and the highest good of all around you. You cease the lower ego's insistence on being right, you recognize that all in this world are part of the whole of All That Is and that each soul has chosen to walk their spiritual path as an aspect of the Infinite One. You also recognize that it is only yourself that requires changing, that one cannot change another. You feel and see in your every day life that life is easier and more harmonious, that your thoughts are clear and in harmony with the world around you.

It is very important to know yourself!

It is when you go out into the world around you that you find yourselves coming back to your inner sanctuary filled with thoughts that you did not carry before. This is when you realize that you have picked up thoughts and feelings that are not rightfully yours to carry. It is very important, we stress again, to know yourself. When you know yourself, you can peacefully stay in your center and will not be moved from this by any external forces. You will know that you truly are walking your path and not following the agenda of another. It always comes back to your daily disciplines, Beloved Ones. You may say, "Well, I am now at a higher frequency level and no longer need to be so diligent" but if you cease your daily disciplines, what happens is that you then begin to flounder in your centeredness within yourselves and find that you are being swayed by the agendas and intentions of others, rather than following your own truth. It then requires a re-dedication once again to yourself and your own chosen path. If you adhere to the daily disciplines and align with your highest truth and Divine Self, your way forward is always made in clarity.

As one gains and radiates more Light, others become attracted to your Light. It is important for this reason, to know yourself, so that you may discern when others want only to take some of your Light from you for their own reasons and purposes. I say to you, if there are question marks within you in regards to requests that are made of you, or confusion or lack of clarity, it is time to take a step back and release the situation until clarity is regained. There is no danger to you by following your own inner counsel, you are always in the right place and space at exactly the right time.

As one gains and radiates more Light, others become attracted to your Light.

You each have your own personal rhythm of greater expansion that occurs when you are processing more of the higher energies than at other times, so it is important to discover when that is, so that you are aware of this and can put this expansive energy to the use of greater potential for yourself and the world in which you live. It is during this time that you are contributing more energy to maintaining the stability of the Earth and all its grids and also to fulfilling your own soul's purpose for being here.

If you find that your personal rhythm of greater expansion occurs during your sleep times, set the intention that you will be working and contributing your Light and energies for the highest good of all before bedtime. If your energies are flowing through you at a higher, more noticeable level during the daylight hours, then this is your time where you can work in unison with your Divine self to bring in and anchor more Light. This is another aspect of knowing yourselves, there are many others, such as being aware of any self sabotaging thoughts and behaviors that may surface from within you after you have spent much time and energy visualizing, affirming or decreeing for that which you desire to experience in your world. Or having thoughts of limitation and doubt and giving up on creative ideas. There are many ways in which these old programs can resurface and it is very important for this reason to become totally aware of self. If you start each day with clarity and knowing of self that is the gauge that you can use when interacting with others so that you know when the energies suddenly change. Then you can take immediate steps to bring yourself back to your own energy by consciously recognizing the new energy is someone else's.

Spend time each day to observe yourself in your actions, thoughts and deeds and correlate these with the events that transpire at later times.

Most of you understand the need to take full ownership of all that occurs for you in your daily lives. You are aware that you are the creator of all that comes into your experience. This is a difficult concept for many to fathom, as the world in which you live does not manifest your thoughts and intentions as quickly as happens in the higher dimensions. It does not happen instantly and so the connection between your thoughts, feelings and intentions is not apparent unless one is aware that this occurs. As you are regaining your Mastery, this awareness becomes easier to grasp. Do spend time each day to observe yourself in your actions, thoughts and deeds and correlate these with the events that transpire at later times. This is where keeping a journal entry each day would be most helpful to you, for just by recording your thoughts and feelings each day, you would be able to look back and say "Aha, I created that!" Becoming the Master of your life can be a most exhilarating experience and journey so make it an adventure!

I would like to continue to address the topic of the current process that is occurring for many of you and that is, alignment and integration with your Divine Self. This is a process set in motion before each of you came into this world for the purpose of not only your ascension but by going through everything that your sisters and brothers are now beginning to go through and experience, you are thereby helping them in their processes, the term used in today's vernacular "been there and done that". Indeed you have, Dear Ones. You are well versed in this process and this is not your first time working in this process. What is so immensely to your credit is that you willingly chose to come here knowing that you would be totally forgetful of your Divine origins. Now, the next step is to reconnect and realign with the Divine being that you truly are. You are coming into your own remembrance.

Becoming the Master of your life can be a most exhilarating experience and journey, make it an adventure!

This, for most of you, will be a natural process rather than a spectacular and sudden expansion of remembrance. For your own highest good and safety, this was what was chosen in order for you to accomplish your tasks without total burn out. You may liken the process of unfoldment within you to the blossoming of a rose as each petal reveals another under it that is also unfolding. All is in Divine order and timing. There is a great order to the Divine Plan, although in truth, it has been in a constant state of adjustment since the Earth has entered into the higher frequencies and a whole new space in the cosmos. This is a totally new experience for all on the planet and all administering systems involved. Much is unfolding, and will continue to unfold. Layer upon layer will be exposed to the truth and the Light and humanity will grow and expand right along with these changes. You are ever the templates of the new, taking the brunt of the new energies and transmuting them by grounding them into the core of the Earth to be dispersed where needed most and enabling humanity as a whole to get on board.

The energies from this point on will become more and more refined and you will find yourselves seeking the quiet place within yourselves in order to process and integrate. The times just ahead of you promise to be filled with more revelation, both personally and collectively. For those of you who have been impatient to 'remember', we say to you, that this way was chosen by you in order to facilitate the raising of the frequency level of the entire planet and all upon her. Each day that you labor in this endeavor brings the Earth and all upon her into greater alignment to the Divine Plan. Keep at the forefront of your thoughts the knowledge that you are co-creating a new Heaven and a new Earth and that this requires that you keep concentrating on the world that you *want* rather than the old paradigm that is breathing its last breath. Business as usual keeping humanity in fear and under control is no longer working and humanity is awakening to the knowledge of their Divine birthright. Giving their power away to others (authority) is no longer acceptable and all are claiming their sovereign right to live a better way.

The current systems that have been in place with their ever increasing demands for more of the energy of humanity will no longer be tolerated and they will crumble and decay.

The next several years will see this taking root in all areas of society and it will happen in a most peaceful and harmonious way. As each person reclaims within themselves their true sovereignty, the weight of the unjust burdens that had been placed upon them will automatically fall away. The current systems that have been in place with their ever increasing demands for more of the energy of humanity will no longer be tolerated and they will crumble and decay. It is happening already everywhere and will become more noticeable as practices and systems that are no longer accepted by the masses. Humanity as a whole is turning away and all is in a state of flux. You, the Lightworkers of the world, are ever the anchors of stability upon the planet and are much needed, for now you are coming into the reason and purpose of your part in the Divine Plan. This will become clearer as the petals unfold and your blossoming occurs, just like the caterpillar who transforms into a beautiful butterfly.

Continue to connect with feelings of joy, happiness, peace and abundance. You have been discovering that all that you really need to feel this way is already all around you, that you have everything you need within you. Change your thoughts and you change your world. Our love for you is ever constant and our assistance ever available.

I want to discuss self value. We see the need from our perspective of the many Lightworkers who need to honor and value themselves. You have worked diligently to develop your abilities and bring forth your Light unto the world, knowing that as you did this, you were blessing the world and everyone around you. You did this by sacrificing the human pleasures that people around you enjoy without thought of consequence. You have purified your thoughts, your bodies, your intentions and motivations. You purified, purified, purified. And still it continues, growing more and more refined, digging deeper and deeper within yourselves, reaching depths that you never knew existed and bringing them forth for your review, acknowledgement, understanding and release.

Change your thoughts and you change your world!

The secret now is to concentrate on feeling love, joy and gratitude. Practice feeling these qualities until it is a constant refrain that takes place without even thinking about it. As you train yourselves to do this, you are changing every cell of your body, transforming it into Light. By focusing on feeling and expressing these qualities, you bring to yourselves more of every good thing in life which will inspire you to express these qualities again and again. For the universe brings to you more of what you focus on. Yes, the world you have been living on has seeming chaos everywhere you turn, but you do have a choice, Dear Ones. You can choose to focus on expressing and manifesting that which you want rather than expressing the thoughts and attitudes of the old dualistic way of being. By making this choice, you are choosing that which is life enhancing and your life will continue to be blessed in many ways.

You will come to the realization that you are the creator in your life and you will see the manifestations of this in the most amazing ways. The universe will open up avenues for you through synchronistic events that will lead you to your highest and greatest good. This is the way of the new world, the ascended world. Begin to bring it into your everyday existence now. Know that the universe is very rich and there is enough for all and not only that, but the universe is like a magic genie who gives to you all you have ever desired.

The secret now is to concentrate on feeling love, joy and gratitude!

Desire greatness, Dear Ones, desire to be the best that you can be. Your soul is ready to take flight into multi-dimensionality and unlimited potential. The very atmosphere around you is supporting you at this time. Visualize yourselves as brilliant beings of Light, golden white Light. At the core of every soul, this is the true essence of being. Your Light body is immortal, incorruptible, desiring greater unification and integration with you. See your radiant self around your physical self each day. This will help to bring it in and anchor it within self.

Use any means available that will keep you connected to this image of your radiant self, feel and express love, joy and gratitude at all times. This is the surest way to full integration. The times ahead are filled with great potentiality. It requires your due diligence and the honoring of your self. Listen always to the voice within. During these times, there are always those upon your world who would take from you the Light that you are by making judgments upon you when you stand in the Light that you are. Just tell yourselves that their opinion of you is not any of your business and move on into greater spiritual expansion. Those who expand themselves into their greater potential are indeed honoring themselves and the Creator. This includes at this time in your history, asking for an energy exchange of money for your services. You still walk upon this world and cannot sustain yourselves from the air alone or keep yourselves warm in the cold winter days by your thoughts alone, you need the energy of money in order to see to your daily needs. There is no dishonor to self by providing services that are truly desired and needed by others in exchange for the energy equivalent of money. The days are not yet upon your world where one can fill their needs instantly by thought alone.

Humanity is far surpassing all previous predictions of what would occur in the world!

As you daily walk your spiritual path, know that you are divinely supported in all of your endeavors, those that are for your highest good. Each of you never walks alone, even in those times when it seems that you are. Never forget this, Beloved Ones. We are with you always.

It has been a stellar time in terms of the signs of things that are yet to come. There are many events that are on the horizon and will become a regular occurrence as the days come and go. There is much speculation as to what is being seen in the skies and as these sightings keep occurring, the people of the world will have to begin questioning what it all means. And in their search for answers, their awakening will occur.

I wish to bring to your attention the confusion that is caused by some who claim that your world is dividing into those who are of higher frequency and those who will be left behind. Please understand, Dear Ones, this is a scenario that might have happened many years ago but did not because there was enough of humanity who had turned to the Light, percentage wise and so this probability came to naught. As we have told you many times, humanity is far surpassing all previous predictions of what will occur in the world and what is now occurring is that the world and everyone on it are moving into uncharted territory, creating the new world as they take each new step and hold the vision of the world they want and desire.

This is what we mean when we say that you are the creators. You are literally creating the new world right now, through your conscious decisions and choices. We ask you to remember this, as there will continue to be those that wish to sway you into fear and another direction that might not be for your highest good. Use discernment, Dear Ones. This is the time it is most sorely needed! As we have stressed before, if you hear something or read something and it creates fear, doubt, worry, confusion or distress in you, this is a sure sign that it is not of the highest Light and truth. Use your own initial reactions as the barometer and you will always be guided to that which is for your highest good.

Use your own initial reactions as the barometer and you will always be guided to that which is for your highest good.

There are many people upon the world right now who are still playing the games of ego and want only fame and the attention it brings them. On the surface, what they bring to the world may seem to sound as the truth and often, much of what they say makes perfect sense, but then this is peppered with glaring untruths that set people into confusion and this is how they capture those who do not remain in their core center and those who do not go within to their heart space to feel the truth. Now is the time to be in observation mode and to follow your heart guidance rather than what someone else might tell you. If your heart says no but your mind says yes, please listen to your heart.

It has been heartwarming for us to observe the efforts of those of you who truly care about what is happening on your world and speaking as one voice and making your calls. This fulfills the universal law that humanity must ask through their own free will before assistance can be given. Your calls are being heard, Dear Ones, and are aligned to the Creator's intent for the Earth and all of her inhabitants. By doing this, you have set the intent that humanity wants the highest outcome for the

Earth and all upon her and do not wish to go on detours that would take them from their path of Light, love and peace. Humanity, the Earth and the Cosmos are in alignment. The glory that humanity is heading into encompasses all who choose to come and when the choices are clearly laid before you, who will not choose the highest outcome?

Each of you is deeply loved and appreciated for choosing the highest outcome not only for yourselves but on behalf of all upon the Earth and the Earth herself. This indicates that you are now moving into world service and that you have successfully passed many tests and initiations to arrive at this point. It also indicates mastery of self and Earthly life and the laying down of the lower ego. You have chosen once again the high road and this has created a corresponding response from the universe. Know that you are blessed beyond measure and that your victory is assured.

If your heart says no but your mind says yes, please listen to your heart!

This is a powerful time for all upon the planet. It is a time of continued cleansing and the refining and the letting go of all that no longer serves, a time of reflection on the direction you wish to travel and a time of awakening to new possibilities and abilities. Many of you have been experiencing a replay of all that you thought had already been purged from you and have been wondering when you would be free of these. Dear ones, this is a completion for you. It might be likened to a bardo experience that happens when a soul departs from Earth; in your case, you have chosen to continue on in your ascension journey while in your physical body so you are experiencing a review of your life lived on the Earth up to this point in time. All is in divine order and we ask you to be at peace about this occurrence. Just allow these thoughts and feelings from the past to pass through you, allow all the feelings of sadness, injustice, grief, indignation and anger to be released. This will be a final purging.

Be patient with yourselves. I know I have said this many times before, but it is necessary to keep repeating it because we notice so many of you being too hard on yourselves. It is a tremendous process that you are going through and it can feel as though it is never ending. The less resistance you make to what comes up, and acknowledge and understand what is occurring, the faster this phase of your ascension process will transpire.

It is a tremendous process that you are going through and it can feel as though it is never ending.

Just allow all of it to pass through you as a detached observer and you will soon be stepping into your new role in alignment with your Divine Plan. This is the reason for the great undercurrent of excitement that you feel. It is the blossoming of all of your possibilities that are beckoning upon the horizon. Go with it! Spend time developing your imagination and live your wondrous fantasies, for they are to become the foundation of your new life upon this planet. The energies at this time are very conducive for dreaming into existence your new way of living.

Relax and enjoy the love, peace, joy and hopeful spirit of this time upon your Planet. Laugh, dance and sing and look into the eyes of each other as you do it, for that is where each soul shines through. Connect with each other on a deeper level. You have learned to shield your heart from the pain of your daily living on a planet that has been inundated with negative thought forms, deeds and activities that have not been for your highest good. It is time now to allow your heart to open to love and the oneness we all are a part of and not be afraid to do so. It requires great courage to make oneself vulnerable in this way but it is what is needed to step into the new world of the Golden Age that is glimmering on the horizon.

As you open your hearts, greater Light comes in, and as this occurs a greater cleansing and purging continues which will lighten your heart and the load you have been carrying for far too long. Smile often and give thanks for all the good things and good people in your life. Gratitude is the attitude that leads to greater abundance. You deserve a cornucopia pouring forth the delicious fruits of your many labors of love. Allow yourselves to feel those precious moments of joy, happiness and well being. May you be blessed in all ways.

The focus now is on maintaining your integrity and keeping yourselves grounded into the core of Mother Earth. Those of you who have been working a long time with the new frequencies and energy are finding that interaction with those who still abide in the un-awakened frequencies a painful exercise in transmutation as they pull your Light and your higher energy from you which you then need to process. We say to you Dear Ones, that this is a part of your task in your everyday lives upon the Earth…it has always been so throughout your Earthly journeys, in this lifetime and other lifetimes that you have lived upon the Earth. You are helpers who came in voluntarily knowing full well how difficult your task of living upon the Earth in your veils of forgetfulness was going to be. You have the great flame of love burning brightly within your hearts and it is this Light that has kept you in the forefront, ever cutting and blazing a trail of Light in order to light the way for those who follow, and follow they shall, Beloved Ones.

The energies at this time are very conducive for dreaming into existence your new way of living.

There are millions of people who are now beginning to awaken to the knowledge and awareness of their higher potential. Your work and sacrifice has made this awakening much easier for these ones and as this happens; the Light you have held for such a long, long time will begin to grow exponentially with each passing day. The more the Light begins to lighten up the Earth, the more people will awaken. The Great Awakening is already occurring and will become more discernible as the weeks, months and years continue. As difficult as it has been for you as the trailblazers in this regard, know that your efforts are now beginning

134

to bear fruit and you will see this in all facets of your daily lives. Much that is transpiring behind the scenes will begin to come out into the open and will create a movement of change upon the face of the planet that will reach the length and breadth of every corner upon your world. There is much to be excited about, Dear Ones, and much more for you to learn and transcend; still, we want you to be very aware that you have done this many times before and this knowledge will become a remembering for you soon.

The more the Light begins to lighten up the Earth, the more people will awaken.

The momentum of the Light has been building in greater waves upon the Earth and is now blending with the great cosmic energies that are inundating every particle of life upon and within the Earth. This Light creates, as you know, much that does not resonate with the Light to come to the surface for your review and release, and this is not a comfortable process but a very necessary one, if you wish to continue on your ascension journey. Trust in this process and call upon us whenever you encounter more friction within you and around you than you can comfortably deal with. We are all standing by, ready to give assistance to you who call upon us and again, we remind you that we must be asked, for this is a universal law. Much assistance can be given to you, but you must first ask. If you could only see clearly the great forces of Light that surround you, you would be dancing all the way through your ascension process! We upon the higher realms feel so very excited to see the leaps and bounds that you are making in your journeys of remembrance and we tell you that you are very near to your goal.

It behooves you to continue in your activism to bring about the changes for the greater good of all by daily working with the Light beings and energies.

Your decrees and affirmations have a greater reach than you can possibly know at this time ... when you repeat a decree, especially more

135

than once, there is a frequency wave that is created and this wave moves out into the atmosphere around the Earth and thereby creates positive change. Even that which could be looked upon as unpleasant change in the end result becomes positive change, for it is all about growth and the coming to greater awareness. I am here to tell you, Beloved Ones, the days of learning lessons through suffering and hardship are coming to a closure, for the new way will be all about learning through and with Grace.

If you could see the great forces of Light that surround you, you would be dancing all the way through your ascension process!

There will be great and joyous leaps in consciousness once this becomes fully established upon the Earth plane. You who are the forerunners are asked to move into this awareness and become the creators and holders of this new way of learning and doing. It no longer has to be hard to create anything you desire, it can be a pleasure and a joy to learn, grow and explore all the new information and knowledge that is now awaiting your explorations. Seek and you shall find!

- Chapter 9 -
The Light That You Are

There are changes taking place within you now that will continue with increasing frequency and regularity. If you have not experienced the high energies running through you before, you will certainly start doing so now. The energies running through your physical body will be unmistakable to you, with many of you vibrating so strongly that you will feel as though you will take off and start flying into the air if they get any stronger. Fear not, Dear Ones, for you that have been prepared for this are now serving as the transducer that we talked about in previous messages. This process means that not only are you holding the Light and anchoring this Light into the crystalline core of the Earth but that your physical body is also transforming and mutating into the crystalline based body. This is the destiny of every human being upon the Earth who has chosen ascension with the Earth, even those who at this time are not even aware that they have made this choice. If you have found your way to be reading these words, you are such a one. Rest assured that with these energies you and all around you, will be changing and indeed, are changing.

All around you now, the hearts of humanity are feeling the Christ energies that are pouring down upon the Earth and all of her inhabitants. The Earth is surrounded by this golden Light and this Light is creating the most wondrous changes within each individual. You who are the trail blazers, the torch bearers, are coming into your own. There will be plenty of work yet to do, for the reason and purpose of your being here at this time in the history of the Earth is now beginning to come into your awareness. You have a great many Guides, Teachers and Angels who surround you constantly and serve you in many ways, whether you are aware of this or not. It behooves you to become attuned to their presence around you. How to do this? Speak out loud to them as though they are visible right in front of you, for truly that is where we are, speak to us of your day, the challenges you are experiencing, the thoughts you have been thinking, the emotions that you have been feeling. When you do this, you acknowledge our presence and it is understood that you desire our input in whatever way is most appropriate. We are joyful in giving you this service, Beloved Ones. Look and listen for our response.

You are 'walking your talk' showing the way by the example of your daily lives which are shining with the radiance of your great spirit.

Many of you will be awakening to the presence of Spirit in the coming months and years and this is a part of the Divine Plan for the Earth and all upon her. There is much that will change as this process unfolds. Know that if you stay centered in the knowledge of the Divine being that you are, knowing that you are loved beyond measure by we of the Family of Light and that you are being guided, assisted and protected in all ways in your daily lives, you will always be doing the right thing at the right time in divine protection. More of you will be banding together in larger groups than ever before to effect greater changes upon your world and are now realizing the great good that can be accomplished as you do this.

You are 'walking your talk' showing the way by the example of your daily lives which are shining with the radiance of your great spirit. This will become more noticeable as the months continue, for your Light will come shining through in all that you do and those around you cannot help but be affected by your Light. Soon this Light as it expands will touch the Light of your sisters and brothers and will ignite and connect all around the world until all there is, is Light. We thank you, Beloved Ones, for all that you are doing, all that you have already accomplished and the great good that is surely taking place upon your planet because you have set foot upon it. We love to be working with you as spiritual comrades, friends and team members. This has created an impetus that is unstoppable and now humankind is turning firmly toward the Light, toward peace, toward a new way of living and being. We rejoice!

This Light as it expands will touch the Light of your sisters and brothers and will ignite and connect all beings around the world until all there is, is Light!

I want to speak with you about the continued application of your intentions for a new way of being upon this world. You are creating this new world in each moment and you are all in the thick of it right now. You have gone deep within and have temporarily disconnected with the outer happenings around you and so you feel as though you are in limbo. Taking actions of any kind at this time seems to require great effort. Our advice, Dear Ones, is to ride this wave and not worry so much about it, this too shall pass. It is a process of redefining yourselves and your world and what it is you truly want.

The next step for you is to start manifesting what you internalized during this process into outer manifestation. It is time to practice your co-creatorship and create, create, create! This is how you come into your Mastership; this is how you create the world you want to experience. Become focused and clear on what it is you want to create, have, be and do, and make it so. Do not rush this process; make it an adventure each day. Play with it and have fun with it. Start each day in joy and gratitude for life and the grand opportunity that is before you. You are supported and loved in all your aspirations, dreams and desires.

The world around you is moving along, seemingly with the same activities and motivations as before but we tell you that this is an illusion those who are losing ground are desperately trying to maintain and it is well that you are not giving these attempts any credence or attention, for as these attempts to distract and dis-empower you continue unabated, those who are just awakening are beginning to see through these ploys. They see these claims for what they really are and that is good news for all. All that is really needed by the people of this world is to stay calm and at peace, and not react to the stories that are being perpetuated continuously. These stories are instantly replaced with more and become ever more laughable to those who can see what is really going on.

Start each day in joy and gratitude for life and the grand opportunity that is before you. You are supported and loved in all your aspirations, dreams and desires!

We see that there are many underground movements occurring to bring about great reforms in government and other institutions. This will continue to grow exponentially as more people join in these movements and add their voices to the demands for positive changes to start taking place. All over the Internet which touches everyone across your world, people are banding together in common purpose and creating these movements for change, for change is upon the face of the Earth in every facet of it. Practice deep breathing each day and accept the changes that are happening. Life is teeming with infinite possibilities and probabilities at this time and choices are being worked out through your connections with your Divine selves.

Trust that the universe is unfolding everything as it should and that you are supported on your journey. You have been key to what is now unfolding all about you. Continue to stand in your Light and maintain your core center, seek that connection within your heart space in your alone times.

I want to discuss the rising energy levels within you. Most of you have been feeling these energies lately and also feeling rather emotional at times as you perform your daily spiritual disciplines. This feeling that you are experiencing is the answering down pouring from the higher realms in response to your calls and petitions to the Creator. This feeling will continue to manifest within you and it indicates that your heart chakra is opening more to the greater energies. This is a very good sign, for when you feel more with your heart, you then also encompass more of your psychic abilities and gifts, the gifts of intuition and inner knowing. This means you are listening and following your own heart. This influx of energy from the higher realms is a way to indicate to you that we are beside you, supporting you and increasing the intensity of your efforts for the highest good of all.

There are so many infinite possibilities and probabilities; the golden gates of opportunity and miracles are wide open!

There are so many diverse energies playing out upon the cosmic fields right now, so many infinite possibilities and probabilities; the golden gates of opportunity and miracles are wide open. You must daily make your calls and set your intentions for the magic and miracles to come into your life and the lives of all upon the Earth. Your work has become even more crucial and important than ever before. Your choosing the Light yet again every day; reinforces the strength and energy of all of the activities of the collective community of Lightworkers. Combined, this energy is a mighty force to be reckoned with. Your combined Light is countering all that is not of the Light. The Light that you are bringing and anchoring into the Earth is creating more of the awakening energies in those around you and thus, more Light radiates out. Truly exciting to behold!

Work with the energies of Mother Earth each day also, Dear Ones, take time to establish a grounding connection to her. This helps the Earth, and also yourselves; you have yet to realize the tremendous good that is being accomplished. The Light you are generating and releasing each day enables and empowers those who are working to bring great reforms and positive changes to your new world to be enfolded in that Light and protected in their endeavors. You are noticing how this is playing out in your everyday lives now.

Nothing can be hidden from the Light of truth any longer, all is being illuminated, ferreted out and is being released for transmutation!

Nothing can be hidden from the Light of truth any longer, all is being illuminated, ferreted out, and is being released for transmutation. You are all making excellent progress, for you are highly motivated to bring about the greatest changes within yourselves. As you do this, you also bring about great changes in those around you. Your Light is being sought by others now who need a place of sanctuary that resonates with their rediscovered greater selves and they will become a mighty seeking force in the near future in your time of reckoning. The third dimensional world is no more in the energy fields around you, it is only being held now in the consciousness of humanity, who is now poised to awaken to their great potential. Once this happens, much progress will take place in every facet of life upon the Earth. Sweeping reforms will rise to the surface of the visions for humanity, and humankind as a whole will take up the reins of self responsibility and self sovereignty in their everyday lives and activities.

There will be more questions brought before all leaders in the world that will require truthful and open answers. Gone are the days that truth can be hidden from the majority of humanity. The impetus from this awakening of humanity's consciousness will revolutionize the world as you know it. Humankind will take back their personal power and will understand that all power lies within. They are realizing that they have a constant connection with the Creator and with the world on which they are manifesting. The limited thinking of previous generations is being opened up to the tremendous possibilities and unlimited potential that exists everywhere in the world and the universe around you. The changes that are taking place are coming fast and furious so we implore you to stay grounded in your physical bodies so that you are fully integrated and can serve as the stabilizing force while many great changes take place.

The impetus from this awakening of humanity's consciousness will revolutionize the world as you know it!

Finally, once again, we remind you to call upon us. Together we can literally move mountains or hold them in place, whatever is appropriate in the days to follow. Every effort you make for the highest good of all is multiplied a thousandfold from the higher dimensions. So it is that we change ourselves and as we do this, change our world.

I want to speak about the deep work that you have been doing within yourselves. We see so much cleansing and purifying of your minds and consciousness occurring. You have come to the point now of greater unification with your Divine self. You have been spending more of your time each day in greater contemplation and unification with all aspects of yourselves that are now coming into alignment. This is excellent, for it means that you are all firmly committed to your ascension process and will dedicate your time, efforts and focus to this.

On the world scene at this time, much is being played out and life on Earth continues to unfold all that must be brought to the attention of each human heart. As this happens, the heart opens to the greater Light and a realization that you are the Creator manifesting upon the Earth; if not you, then who? For it is you who is creating the great changes upon the Earth with each choice and decision that you make, by each action you take, with each breath you take and each thought that you think. It is beginning to sink in, that along with the opening of your spiritual gifts and talents, comes the self responsibility to create the highest and the best for all concerned, so that everyone may enjoy peace upon your planet and also take part in the joy of life in its every expression.

At the level of spirit, all hearts are uniting and working in unison!

All about you life moves forward, even though it appears to be the opposite. Underneath all the seeming opposites a greater union is taking place and Oneness is occurring. At the level of spirit, all hearts are uniting and working in unison, it is now only a matter of time before the greater Light within all hearts explodes within and encompasses all within its radiance. The wheel of life turns as all is brought to a Oneness of life, and a greater understanding of this is now coming forth. There is a connection that exists beyond all time, all borders, all beliefs, all races and the threads of Light are coalescing into a greater and greater Whole. The radiance that emanates from the Earth is reaching further and further out into the cosmos and the brilliance of spaceship Earth is becoming brighter and brighter in the Heavens.

You are being guided to what you need at each moment in order to facilitate greater growth so that your heart opens in an ever greater unfolding like the petals of a rose, a beautiful rose of purity and pristine impeccability. All that used to hold your attention is now falling away and you are beginning to discern that which is of importance on your journey and focusing more upon that. We have noticed a great determination and focus upon that which you want. You have been contemplating and refining your 'wish list', even if you don't think so at this time. It is readily apparent to the higher realms, Dear Ones, of the brilliance of your Light. We understand that growth is not always pleasant whilst going through it, but in retrospect, the value of it is seen, understood and appreciated and so it is with this process.

The planet Earth has opened up to the whole universe and all of Creation rejoices and celebrates this momentous occasion. There are ceremonies of joy and celebration taking place within all sectors of this universe and beyond. There is much happiness and thanksgiving within the hearts of all who have waited for this time through the eons. Humankind has once again joined with the rest of the universe and much that was not known before will be coming to the Light of awareness. That which was a mystery will be coming up for enlightenment, clarification and completion. This will be an ongoing process and one that is filled with great excitement for all. When humanity begins to understand the enormity of what has transpired, the greater awakening will occur and, life will become enjoyable, meaningful and sacred to everyone on the planet once again. This is a glorious time for all upon the Earth and indeed to all of Creation. The remembrance of the glory and majesty that you are will come to awareness in trickles that will build to a great stream of consciousness and this will bless the Earth and all upon her. Your places in the annals of the history of this cycle are clearly written and you are honored, appreciated and admired for the great work you are doing.

It is now only a matter of time before the greater Light within all hearts explodes within and encompasses all within its radiance!

Much is transpiring in the events and happenings in the world and you are all prepared for it. You have been taking part in meetings beyond your sleep state and you know your part in the times to come. Many revisions have been and continue to take place because your intent to create changes to any dire predictions that have been previously made continues to come into effect. In other words, Dear Ones, you are creating your world as we go along. This is a wonderful facility that you have been developing; for as you read of trends and predictions, you effect changes to counteract that which has been given and the world is a better place because of it.

There are some Earth changes that might take place and it behooves you to stock up on essential items for your daily needs as there could be a possibility of supply routes being blocked for a time. We are not advocating running out and buying up everything in sight, what we are saying is that you anticipate what your needs would be during temporary shortages and take steps now to ensure you are taken care of, in the event that this should be necessary. It is amazing how little you really need during times of shortages, only that which takes into consideration hygienic needs and basic food stuffs.

When humanity begins to understand the enormity of what has transpired, the greater awakening will occur and, life will become enjoyable, meaningful and sacred to everyone on the planet once again!

The world is poised on the brink of several events that will remove forever that which has been holding humanity as a whole back from their rightful place in the universe and the overall scheme of things. It will come as a shock to many people that they were enslaved when they thought they were free and sovereign, and this will be a quick and rude awakening but will leave no lasting effects and will not be harmful. Life upon your planet is ready to move to the next step and all is in readiness for this occurrence to take place. The energies that have been coming through your atmosphere have been preparing humanity for this next step. You have all been receiving energies that have enabled you to be able to withstand what is to come forth.

We have been working with all of you and some of you are beginning to remember instances of this. Know that you no longer go into any situations with blinders on; for you are consulted at every turn in the direction the Divine Plan and its many facets takes. There have been and will continue to be revisions made to stay on track and on task to Creator's true purpose and intent for the times ahead. All is working accordingly. Nothing that takes place is by accident; all is by design and Divine Intent.

Stay true to yourselves and let all your decisions be made from the area of your heart space. You will know that this is the right way for you to go by the feeling of lightness and rightness that you experience and feel. Your Divine self is always guiding you to make the right choices in Divine timing. All unfolds as it should for your particular part in this Plan. You are exactly where you should be and you are much needed there. As the great Light Beacons that you are, you are the anchors for the energies of Light and stability that is required at this time. For those of you who have been wondering why you are where you are, this is the reason, even though you have felt alone and unsupported by those around you. This will start changing in the times ahead and you will become more valued and you will no longer feel as though you are invisible.

All unfolds as it should for your particular part in this Plan. You are exactly where you should be and you are much needed there!

Your input will be sought by those around you and all of a sudden, what you have stood for all these years will begin to sink in to those around you. You will begin to go into action to fulfill your part in the Divine Plan. Know, Dear Ones, that there is nothing to fear but fear itself and that you are ever walking a path of Light to the next step in your evolvement. Keep ever onward and moving forward and all will be revealed in the fullness of time. Seek inner counsel each day and you will stay in peace and harmony throughout the coming times. You have but to call on any of us and we will assist you. Know that you are, each of you, beloved of the Ascended realms and that we work together in unison.

The energies have intensified and you will find yourselves feeling empowered and fully energized, or feeling confused, unfocused and tired. Either way, the ascension process continues and you keep moving more into alignment with Galactic Center. The dimensions are merging and you are out of the third and passing quickly through fourth. The fifth dimension waits, shimmering radiantly with untold possibilities. Wonder and magic is afoot and long forgotten magical kingdoms are and have been, returning to give assistance at this time. The age of magic, rituals and ceremonies, and living authentically is now upon you.

You can do anything! You can accomplish anything you desire, so dream your dreams and dream BIG!

The field is open for all possibilities and imagination is the key to the kingdom that lies before you, awaiting your participation. So much yet to traverse to reach this magical land, yet it is only a breath away. Much will be accomplished energetically within you and many of you will have wondrous experiences as you go within. Some of you will just awaken one morning and remember yourselves in totality. Then the magic begins, then the Light will encompass the entire planet and radiate out to the cosmos in gratitude, love and appreciation for the gifts of the Spirit that were given and remembered.

There is so much beauty that awaits the notice of humanity; so very much that is changed already all about you. As the energies increase, you will begin to notice these subtle and beautiful manifestations with greater frequency. Stay centered and calm in the storm tossed seas that rock to and fro as the great changes start taking place as humanity is released from the confines of the illusion that kept the majority from knowing how very limited their magnificent selves had been confined. Feel this expansion and practice this feeling each day. You can do anything! You can accomplish anything you desire, so dream your dreams and dream BIG!

It is all about expansion on all levels of your being. Taking time to connect to the Earth and nature will help you stay grounded while connecting to the immenseness of the beauty that is within you. Breathe deeply and often in slow, rhythmic breaths in cycles of seven, letting the breath touch right down to your root chakra. This practice in itself gives a great boost in energy and clarity and will leave you feeling invigorated. Step lightly upon the Earth and walk in harmony with all that is about you. Seek the hidden kingdoms everywhere you look, they desire to develop a relationship with you but need to trust that it will be reciprocated with the utmost integrity and responsiveness.

The world you see before you is undergoing transformation on all levels of existence. All is in a state of flux. One's truth is changing from one moment of existence to the next.

There is so much to learn, to know and discover. Seek to learn and grow in the new environment that you have created. What was within is now manifesting outwardly and your abilities are growing exponentially. Soon you will be communicating with all the wondrous beings that have walked at your side. You will see them, know them and remember them. Great joy awaits all those who believe!

The world you see before you is undergoing transformation on all levels of existence. All is in a state of flux. One's truth is changing from one moment of existence to the next. This is so for every human being upon the Earth, and every sentient being who lives in symbiosis with All That Is. As the Earth reflects to you what you are experiencing, a greater and greater cleansing is occurring and much change is transpiring. Humankind's consciousness is expanding daily, all are undergoing deep levels of self analysis and reflection and coming to the truth of their selves and acting upon it.

This is painful for many of you but the end result will see peace re-established upon the entire planet. Now is the time to go with this flow and experience fully what comes up for you, as it is needs to be addressed and balanced within you. The winds of change are upon you, release what is necessary in order that you may stand steady and set sail upon the storm tossed seas. Do not waste time in endless regrets as

150

realizations come upon you, simply experience them and move on, ready for the next wave. You are surfing your way to freedom, Dear and Beloved Ones!

Do not waste time in endless regrets as realizations come upon you, simply experience them and move on, ready for the next wave!

All across the face of the planet these changes are creating and forcing the old ways and paradigms to dissolve into oblivion. The dimensions are shifting and in a state of flux so it is very important to concentrate and focus upon what you want, not your regrets, your pains, your sorrows, your struggles. All of those are just a dream from which you are all awakening. Take heart in this and gather your strength about you. Know that we are always available to give you solace and assistance, as we have always stated. We hear your every thought and experience with you your every anguish and sorrow. We dry your tears, Beloved Ones, and do our utmost to lift you up and help you to remember the mighty beings of Light that you truly are.

Understand, Dear Ones, the new way of living is dawning. Can you feel it within yourselves? Can you see that your understanding of yourselves and those around you has been undergoing radical changes? You are more willing to let go of ego based desires and intentions and are allowing the basic truths of yourselves to unfold. You are the transmitters of love! You have held this great and powerful force within your entire being through millennia of being accosted at every turn because of the great Light that you are in actuality and you forgot the glory that is your Divine birthright. Now, that knowledge is returning, as you release and let go of all that no longer serves you. The end result of all this deep introspection shall be the untold joy of freedom!

Continue to help your sisters and brothers as they continue to be buffeted by the winds of change. It will begin to feel tedious to you because of the frequency of events that continue to transpire. We ask you to remember the whole picture of the Great Divine Plan for the Earth and all of her inhabitants. The changes within humanity's consciousness is now increasing daily, more people are awakening to the realization that they are so much more than they previously believed and that they are deserving of so much more than has been their lot. This realization is powering these individuals forward and they are speaking their truths with increasing frequency. By doing so, they are enabling their neighbor to do the very same. This impetus cannot be turned back and will continue to propel events forward to establish a better way upon your planet.

We want you to remember the great resource that is available to you and that is our help, guidance, insight and assistance.

We are working unceasingly with you and we ask that you begin to accept this and start consciously communicating with us each day. We realize you are busy and distracted by all that you are processing but we want you to remember the great resource that is available to you and that is our help, guidance, insight and assistance. You are always enfolded in the wings of love and protection. Compassion flows to you at this time in the history of your world, the ending of the old and the birthing of the new, which you and we from the Ascended realms have been working together on for millennia. Keep on keeping on, Beloved Ones!

- Chapter 10 -
You Are Serving the Divine

I wish to speak with you in regards to the diverse energies and the expression of these energies at this time. As the Light intensifies as it streams down upon the Earth from the cosmos and enters the atmosphere of the Earth, it enters into the auric field of all living things and begins its great work of purification and alignment to the higher frequencies of consciousness. For those who have been working with intent to raise their frequency levels, this will translate into feelings of joy and expansiveness. For those who are just awakening to these concepts, this is translating into expression at the levels of human ego, as the newly awakened ones take on their newly acquired knowledge. In this new awareness, they feel that they must teach and change others around them. This can sometimes require great patience from those who have been at this work for many, many decades.

The very energies themselves are harbingers of a new order of things. Where once people were afraid to speak up for themselves and their rights in all the situations of their lives, they are now realizing that the speaking of their truths is the only way they can be their authentic selves. By living their highest truths and honoring the presence of the Infinite One within them, they honor this presence within their own being and consciousness. They realize the truth of the old adage, "To thine own self be true" no matter another's opinion on any given subject. There are as many differing opinions as there are people and what is important in such a scenario is to always follow that which is in your own heart, for that is what is true for you. Pleasing others in order to be acceptable to them is no longer viable in the new energies, for then you are not living authentically the life you have chosen for yourself.

Gone are the days of acquiescing to others in any facet of your lives. Yes, if you see there is wisdom in their counsel, by all means agree with it and take appropriate action. But in these new energies, one must always be true to self and what is true for you may not be so for another. This is where great patience comes in and the quality and art of detachment. For the one who has mastered their emotions, there is no need to justify their actions, words or deeds in any way. These ones realize their right as sovereign beings, that they are fully responsible for every one of their words, deeds and actions. It is not required to follow the dictates of another as long as one takes full responsibility for themselves. Everyone upon the planet is a mighty being of Light and has a right to live their life in the true authenticity of their being.

All contribute to the unified field of consciousness with their own unique blend of energies and gifts that no one else can contribute.

The path of Light upon this planet was not blazed by the many but by those who followed the inner promptings and dictates of their own hearts, their own sense of truth and rightness of being. In unity consciousness, there is the honoring of each being's right to experience and follow their inner counsel in all things. All contribute to the unified field of consciousness with their own unique blend of energies and gifts that no one else can contribute. In this way, all are important in the overall scheme of things. Let no one diminish your Light, Dear Ones.

Many of you have been releasing and adjusting, trying to integrate all the changes taking place within your own bodies and in the world around you. Most of you are feeling like lightening rods at this time, walking around in high vibration at all times. Be sure to drink a lot more water when this is happening as this helps keep the energies moving

155

more fluidly through your systems. Some of you are forgetting to do this.

There is a great influx of energy coming in and this will continue for many years to come and you will have a chance to integrate the changes taking place within you for a space of time before the next influx, and this is how ascension happens, one step at a time in order to take all of humanity into ascension with the Earth. Each time one of you raises your vibration, you help raise the vibratory level of everyone on the planet.

Each time one of you raises your vibration, you help raise the vibratory level of everyone on the planet!

Many issues and long unresolved problems are coming up for review, resolution and release. This is going to continue occurring as the days go by, for it is necessary that all energies that are not of the highest Light be resolved in order to let more Light in. It is a time of much human drama as interpersonal relationships make adjustments along with all the bodily adjustments. You are all helping by trying to be mirrors for each other so that this can occur, so that all core issues within each person can finally be released once and for all.

The Earth is also continuing in her birthing process and her metamorphosis is proceeding in the same manner as it is for her inhabitants, with waves of movements and changes that are occurring on a consistent basis. There is much turmoil within the tectonic plates and there will likely be more upheavals taking place on the surface. This is part of a chain reaction that is inter-related under the surface of the planet. All of this is taking place with the least amount of destruction to humanity that can possibly occur.

You will notice that communication between yourselves and others takes on a deeper, more heartfelt connection. This will create more understanding between all people and in turn, will continue to raise the frequency level of everyone on the planet. More people will express the state of joy and this will continue the process, for the more joy that one feels, the greater and higher the vibratory level. The end result we expect is that all are happy and living in harmony. There is however, still more work on yourselves that will continue until the process is complete.

Know that all is in Divine Order and that there will come a time when there is peace at last, both within and without, and then humanity as a collective consciousness will finally experience the joy and happiness that is long overdue for all.

There will come a time when there is peace at last, both within and without, and then humanity as a collective consciousness will finally experience the joy and happiness that is long overdue for all.

Much is transpiring in your daily lives. You are being called upon to let go of all that no longer serves you and sometimes this is not readily apparent to you consciously. Trust that where you are now is exactly where you should be and allow the transformation that is occurring within you to take place. There are no accidents and you are being guided by your Divine self to be in the right place and time for your part in the Divine Plan to activate for your life and for the Earth.

Take time to nurture yourselves in these difficult and challenging times. Open yourselves to receive the higher energies that are continuously pouring down upon the Earth and all upon her. In order to do this, listen to the still, small voice within you. Be alert to synchronicities that occur each day around you. Observe the messages of the universe that are being sent to you each day. The answers to your questions come through those who act as mirrors for you in order to enable you to find your way along your path. Trust that you always receive what is needed at the right moment in order to move you to your next step.

Focus on feeling the love of the unconditional heart of God within your own heart space and radiate it outwards to bless all around you.

Practice the Golden Rule and live your life with impeccability, integrity and honesty. You have much to give to the world and to your individual community, which you have already been doing just by being who you are and standing in your Light and your truth. Continue on your inward journey to connect with your Divine self and know that the time is *now* for the connection to be made.

Practice the Golden Rule and live your life with impeccability, integrity and honesty!

Aspire to greater things and think BIG, even if your logical mind tells you that what you desire cannot be possible. In the higher realms, there is no such thing as impossible, only a solution to be found and implemented. There has been a focus on relationships for many of you and this will continue to play out until all is balanced and resolved for the highest good of all concerned. Always expect the highest outcome in all things and it shall manifest for you. Decree and intend your highest vision and then allow it to blossom into manifestation in your daily life.

This is a time of much releasing, relinquishing and the re-evaluating of your dreams, aspirations and expectations. Many events will keep occurring to distract you from this focus of connecting to your higher truth. You will have to apply great discipline to move past all illusions into the greater truth and meaning of your life and why you are here at this time. Your spiritual gifts come forth each time you make inroads into releasing all within you that is not conducive to the path of Light that you have been on and as you do this, you bless all with your presence.

It is a time of plodding ahead, determination set firmly within you as the changes and transformations occur within you and around you. You may feel as though it is never ending, but there will come a time when you will know that you have accomplished the goal of shedding all that has been holding you back from shining the great Light that you are. No longer will you be hindered by old patterns and concepts that do not serve your highest and best outcome. Keep on keeping on, Dearest Hearts, and know that on this journey, you never walk alone.

Always expect the highest outcome in all things and it shall manifest for you.

Do not give up! You are still going through the process of wringing all that no longer serves you from your minds, bodies and spirits. The Great Work has now begun in great earnestness. All is being cleansed, healed, revealed, and transmuted, for not only your individual selves are involved in this process, but all upon your dear planet. There is much that you are learning about yourselves, each other and the world around you as this happens. The great secret during this time is to forgive yourselves and others in all things and to realize that underlying all experiences is the great force of love.

Cultivate this feeling on a daily basis. Create or find mantras, decrees, invocations and affirmations that daily inspire you to greater heights of Creator love and manifest this within your heart chakra. Spend much time focusing upon this chakra within your body. You may even lie down upon your bed and gently tap your hand on your heart region as a way to focus and feel this space. This location in your body is the gateway to greater things. All must pass through this gateway to be sanctified and balanced before you can enter the new dimension that now lies before you, awaiting your notice.

There is a need for you to drink even greater amounts of pure, clean water each day. This is one of the most basic and important things that you can do to facilitate this vertical growth that you are now going through. Another is deep breathing exercises. Practice daily grounding into the Earth in whatever way works best for you and attune to Mother Earth so that you are at one with her. In this way, you will always be informed of what is occurring and what is about to occur. Observe nature all around you. Learn to experience being in the moment by enjoying simple things around you. Everywhere you look, life is burgeoning into full bloom and there is much to discover.

The great secret during this time is to forgive yourselves and others in all things and to realize that underlying all experiences is the great force of love!

You are the carriers of the love frequency and now is the time to radiate this love to everyone around you wherever you may go. Let your Light shine in its brilliance. Smile often and laugh in joy, for this is a most exhilarating time of life and living upon the Earth. This is what you were made for; this is the time for which you came. Feel the joy of life coursing through your veins and dance if you want to! You are as one with the Creator experiencing these moments, feel the exhilaration of this Presence within you and allow the experience. It is time to feel and BE, rather than rationalizing and analyzing. Enjoy each moment.

Sleep whenever the need comes upon you and listen to the inner promptings of your body. Become attuned in all ways with everything around you and learn to feel this within you. Your own inner guidance system is coming online and onboard and it is now the time to use it. There is so much wisdom and knowledge that is waiting to burst forth into manifestation from within you now and all is in alignment for this to occur.

It is the time of great cleansing upon the Earth and within every being upon her. This is a momentous task, as you can well imagine, for it requires that your individual support teams work with you constantly to assist and facilitate the greatest amount of growth and expansion in your consciousness. This they do so that you may quickly take your rightful place as the multi-dimensional beings that you truly are. This growth can take many forms and lessons, and oftentimes, leaves question marks in your minds as to what is actually happening. Trust that all is as it should be and connect deeply into your hearts, to get in touch with your deepest truth and all will be well.

We understand that as you are being tested by this cleansing, many emotions surface that you believed had already been dealt with and so it may seem as if no progress is being made. We say to you, Dear Ones, that much progress is being made if you could but see the whole picture. Trust that all that is occurring for you right now is exactly what should be occurring and feel everything out with your deepest heart space; for in everything, love is the answer. Find your balance and equilibrium by intending the highest and best outcome and give it over to your Divine self. Have faith and trust that this is part of the greater plan for your life in these changing times.

You are the carriers of the love frequency and now *is* the time to radiate this love to everyone around you wherever you may go!

Some of the feelings that you have been experiencing are coming from a different aspect of yourselves that has been re-united within your Monad. You have taken on the unresolved issues of this aspect of your greater self in order to bring equilibrium and integration within your Divine self. This is the focus for everyone at this time, to bring together all that was lost and separated because of former lifetimes and their happenings, which created such divisions. Now is the time for all of these to come together in peace, harmony and great healing. If you have experienced much emotion and then find yourselves feeling the need for much sleep, know that this is part of the process of re-integration. Just go with the flow of what your mind and body feels and act upon it.

Your bodies are cleansing and releasing much, both physically, emotionally, mentally and as just stated, multi-dimensionally. In time, this will facilitate the total integration with your Divine self and you will begin to manifest only the very highest qualities of your Divine self in your embodiment upon the Earth. When you perceive yourself as doing this, then that is a sign that you are fully integrating with your Divine self and your true gifts shall come forth to bless all those around you. I wish to state that this is happening to a great many of you at this time. Much work has been done and more of this unfoldment will continue. Just keep in mind, Beloved Ones, that no matter where you go, you must take your self with you so it behooves you to face your starkest truths as soon as possible and move on.

No matter where you go, you must take your self with you so it behooves you to face your starkest truths as soon as possible and move on.

All around you, this theme is being played out. It is not readily apparent on the surface of things, as humanity is not used to disclosing their less than Light tendencies to the world around them; nevertheless, know that this is being played out in every corner of the world. Keep your focus on the Great Work you have come to do, and as soon as possible after dealing with your core issues, get back to it. We see and understand that this process can be difficult, as these issues that come up are your deepest ones and inevitably distract you from your ongoing task of anchoring and holding your Light upon the planet. We also see that the majority of you are succeeding in your re-focusing because deep within, you realize the reasons for this and how important it is at this time. I know that it is easy to say and much harder to do, Beloved Ones, your challenge is to let go and let God. Let go of the personality ego self and intend your Divine self into everyday manifestation in your life. On a personal level for each of you, this is the greatest task at this time.

We wish for you to know at this juncture that all you have to do is say, *"I ask for assistance in overcoming, releasing and clearing the challenges that are before me now, gaining the lesson and the wisdom, and moving forward in confidence"* and you will see an improvement in your lives very soon after. You are loved so very much!

You have been clearing from you all that you are not and this is an ongoing process and will continue unabated until your Light body has fully descended into your physical body system. It has been a difficult time for many of you as you continue to wrestle with your own self and sense of identity, not only for yourself but also those that are closest to you. Please understand, Beloved Ones, that there is a great deal of energies intermingling at this time, from the past, present and future. All is coming together, all that needs to be addressed, acknowledged, observed and released. Do not despair; rather, realize that in the overall plan, this is actually a very positive occurrence. As you release what you are not and let it go, more Light takes its place within you and this is how you are making inroads on your spiritual journey.

Keep firmly in mind that your thoughts are powerful!

It is very important at this time, Beloved Ones, to keep firmly in mind that your thoughts are powerful and that what you focus on will manifest for you, so it behooves you to keep your thoughts turned to the positive, to the highest vision and highest outcome in all situations. We realize that this is very difficult to do when you are in the throes of releasing. Know that you have an incredible amount of support and that you are never alone. Your spiritual guides, teachers and angels work unceasingly with you, inspiring you from on high, uplifting your spirits when you grow weary, and helping you to sleep so that we can better assist in the adjustments to your physical bodies. The changes within you are happening at a much faster rate now and those of you reading this book are at the forefront of the metamorphosis taking place within you and the Earth. As you change, Mother Earth also changes and you help each other along the path to ascension.

We advise, as before, great amounts of pure, clean water, more than adequate rest and as much time outdoors as is possible, for these three things do much to restore and maintain your equilibrium at this time. Many of you are feeling the desire to bring your physical bodies into greater health and performance. You are responding to the urges of your Divine self as you are being prepared to embody your higher consciousness and to become more multi-dimensional than at present. It is a challenging time for everyone and also, the most exciting time to be alive upon this planet at this most significant turning point in her history. Mother Earth is truly grateful for the energies of love and healing that are being sent to her. If you are one who feels emotional as you decree the Invocation to the Cosmic Light, we wish for you to realize that what you are experiencing is the immense gratitude of Mother Earth as you do this and this gratitude expresses through you as the welling of tears and choking of voice. The more you are attuned to Mother Earth, the greater the feeling of empathy with her.

You are being prepared to embody your higher consciousness and to become more multi-dimensional than at present.

Keep on keeping on, Dearest Hearts, and rest assured that your efforts are not in vain and that what you are accomplishing far surpasses all former expectations. The Light within each human heart that turns on adds to the momentum and is having a far reaching effect. Remember that where you are situated on Earth at this time is exactly where your Light is needed and those in your communities are blessed for it, whether they are consciously aware of it or not. The time of the Lightworker is coming to the fore. The Great Work has begun and we of the Family of Light are so very excited by all the possibilities and probabilities that lie waiting to manifest upon your world. Take heart and listen to the still, small voice within you, for this is your greatest ally at this time. We stand always ready to be of assistance to you

The times that are now upon you require great focus and concentration on the Light that you are. You are being tested in many diverse ways and much of this comes from the area of discernment, for there are many things taking place in your lives that have you wondering if you are 'losing it'. We say to you, Dear Ones, that the veils are lifting and all that is illusion in your lives is being shattered. What you are now seeing is the effects of this, painful as it may be. Realize that it is all for a higher purpose, a greater movement into the higher dimensional reality. You may feel that this is not so, that you are stuck and wallowing in the mud of the past and the illusions of the present and will never see the Light you have worked so faithfully and diligently for.

The growth of awareness within a soul comes by experiencing the nature of duality so that a clear choice can be made in the direction of the Light.

Beloved Ones; keep up the good work by raising your vibratory frequency each day. You know by now that decreeing, mantras, affirmations and meditation serve to attract the higher energy flow to you and through you to the center of the Earth and that this is the Great Work for which you came. Do not give up hope of a better life for yourselves and all of your loved ones, including those that are testing you greatly in this present moment. They are also awakening to their greater potential, and as you know, this is sometimes accomplished through friction and tension. The growth of awareness within a soul comes by experiencing the nature of duality so that a clear choice can be made in the direction of the Light.

You have already chosen this path and have been embarked upon it for many, many lifetimes. This is the lifetime where the momentum of all that you have strived for is upon you now, this is the moment in cosmic time when all the great forces of Light are gathering and integrating into the wholeness of Oneness, into remembrance of all that you truly are. This process is ever unfolding and your task now is to stay the course, no matter what. Daily send your blessings of love and Light to those in your immediate circle of influence and have patience with their actions and activities. All is not as it seems, for there are a great many forces at work in each situation and it is being brought up for resolution, healing and integration with your Divine selves.

Try to stay centered within the core of your being and keep life simple. The less distraction you have in the form of the old paradigm thinking, concepts and expectations, the easier it will be for you to move forward by leaps and bounds. Be your kind selves to others and realize that many times the problems you encounter or even create, stem from the fact that your inner sight and vision is unfolding and therefore, you 'see' what is evolving around another person. When you mention what you see to them, they react with anger and denial because they are not yet used to going within and seeing all these facets of themselves with the greatest honesty and introspection. The times that are upon you will have the effect of facilitating this process within each individual upon the planet.

Daily send your blessings of love and Light to those in your immediate circle of influence and have patience with their actions and activities.

You are the bright Lights that are raising the Earth and all upon her to ever higher dimensional levels. Now is the time to join together in groups working for the highest good of All That Is. Seek out and join those with whom you resonate and work together each day to add higher energies in a stable way for the highest good of all. These people, leaders who have been training for these times, will be coming into your knowledge and what is hoped by we of the Family of Light is that you will all join together in a greater unified force and focus for the highest good of all. You, Beloved Ones, are the great changers of destiny. You came into the world during these very times to be paradigm busters, illusion breakers, veil lifters and heart awakeners. This means that you have had to experience all of these personally in order to accomplish this.

You are all on your right paths, Dear Ones, know this and do not give up or doubt yourselves. Stay centered within your Light and your great love for Creator. Daily seek counsel with your own Divine Light and listen to the still, small voice within you. All is well and everything is perfect. Say this to your selves each day and it becomes so!

You came into the world during these very times to be paradigm busters, illusion breakers, veil lifters and heart awakeners!

The changes continue to take place both within your personal lives and reflected out into your world. All about you, people are experiencing events that take them by surprise and shock them into re-evaluating what it is they stand for and what they want from their life. As these events take place, a time of stress and tension is experienced and this becomes conducive to the process of going deep within to discover more about one's true state of being. The time for honest evaluation and introspection is upon you.

This is a time to simplify your lives so that the least amount of stress can touch you. The new energies keep bringing up all that which is not really your true self that has been harbored deep within your subconscious mind. These thoughts and programs have been methodically planted there by the society you have lived in and which you have been led to believe was the truth. All of it is being questioned now and brought to the surface. For the majority of the lightworkers, this process is almost completed and the end of this trying time is in sight.

We see and understand how difficult it has been for you to maintain your focus on holding and standing in your Light, for the events in your lives have brought about great distractions. Many times your energies have been so taken up with these events, that it was all you could do to keep one foot in front of the other as you walked your daily path. The key here is to connect with your higher mental body and remember that the goal is to bring in your Divine self. It is through the great power of love that all can be overcome. One must cast aside the personality ego self and earnestly desire the manifestation of the Divine being that you truly are.

167

Therefore, we say to you that this process is taking place. As you connect with your desire to manifest as your Divine self, so shall more Light enter within your 5 body system and the great cleansing will continue. All that is unlike your Divine self is now in the process of transmutation. Like a phoenix, you shall rise from the ashes of the fires of purification to emerge as the Divine being that you truly are. As you do this, you raise the Light quotient of every soul upon the planet.

Know that you are divinely assisted and supported in every way possible; all we ask is that you remember to ask for assistance each day. This process is necessary in order to move the Earth and all upon her up to the next rung on the ladder of ascension. Stay strong, Beloved Ones, and believe in yourselves, for you are the great Light and hope of your world.

Like a phoenix, you shall rise from the ashes of the fires of purification to emerge as the Divine being that you truly are. As you do this, you raise the Light quotient of every soul upon the planet!

Long has it been since you have felt good in your daily lives, for all about you now, the changes and transformations are taking place. Your bodies are enduring a great pressure and this translates into high emotions and eruptions that leave you feeling as though you have not gained an iota of Light quotient for a very long time. Dear Ones, this is the ascension process, this is how your physical, mental, emotional and spiritual bodies become purified so that you may rise into the higher dimensions. In days of long ago, this was accomplished by living a solitary life with full focus on this process; in the current time this process is occurring within each human upon the planet and it is happening continuously without ceasing. The only way out is to go within, for the answer to greater comfort and ease lies within your being.

As you strive to reconnect to the balanced being you once were, before the advent of the greater energies that are now being streamed upon the Earth, remember that you are in the forefront of this process. You are the volunteers who chose to come at this time to go through the same process as every being upon the Earth. The goal is to rise up and increase the Light quotient within yourselves and also the mass consciousness field. This you are doing, even though you seemingly have had no input in adding to the Light quotient, for you yourselves are the Light. By participating in this process, you are overcoming all the illusions of humanity and will soon stand in the full Light of your greater selves. Take heart, Dear Ones, and be compassionate to yourselves and others. This is a very testing time for all upon the planet and much of the accumulated dross of the ages is being released, transmuted and transformed.

Stay strong, Beloved Ones, and believe in yourselves, for you are the great Light and hope of your world.

You know intrinsically that this is the service you came to perform and that somehow you would instinctively work your way through it, and you are! Hold to your visions of the highest good and greatest outcome for the Earth and all upon her and it shall be so. Even if for just five minutes every day, invoke the Light of God that never fails and send it through yourselves out into the world around you, to heal and bless all within your radius of influence. This helps more than you can imagine, for it is your Light that is the grounding force upon the Earth and that Light is very much needed. Stay the course, Dearest Hearts, keep ever at your task, put in your best efforts each day. That is all that can be asked of you in these times. Your intentions are more powerful than you can fathom so practice setting your intentions on paper and repeat these, preferably at the same time each morning. This will assist in bringing to you that which you truly desire and will also assist you in leaving behind all that does not resonate with the greater Light coming through you.

In all things practice moderation and strive for equilibrium at all times. All that you have been enduring is serving a greater purpose than you can comprehend at this time in the Earth's history. When the timing is right, you will remember that purpose and be filled with a joy that knows no bounds! The Light Bearers are leading the way, cutting the path for those who follow. You knew it would not be easy, yet here you are, almost through it! Keep up the excellent work, and shine that great and ever increasing Light that you are!

- Chapter 11 -
Hold Steady the Vision

As you travel through the confusing energies, know that what is required of you is the steadfast adherence and fidelity to the Light that you serve. There is much that is coming before you now that tests you and is keeping you from moving forward in leaps and bounds. This is a process that requires your patience, Dear Ones, for before you can leap your next step in a single bound, you must first eliminate from all levels of your body and being all that is not of the Light that you are.

Many of you are being tested by watching your beloved family members struggle with challenges that seemingly come out of nowhere and that require moving forward step by step in a situation that was not of their own making. Know that this too, is for a higher purpose and without the current situation in their lives, they would not have the opportunity to gain inner strength and insight into the inner workings of their minds, hearts and souls. All that comes up for them is that which must be addressed, acknowledged and faced with courage and the willingness to look into their shadow selves and those of others.

The Great Cleansing continues and will step up in intensity, so it behooves you to be prepared so that you meet whatever it is with calmness and equilibrium. Your connection with your Divine self is most important right now. Spend as much time every day as you can cultivating a relationship with your Inner Being. Go within as often as necessary to maintain your equilibrium. You are the beacons of Light and as your Light grows, it expands further in radius and you ignite others to awaken to a higher consciousness. The more Light you carry, the more people are exposed and begin to awaken and the greater impact is made. This is serving in the most practical capacity at this time.

Remember that you are, first and foremost, an Ambassador of Creator, moving through your daily activities and experiencing life as a human aspect of Creator. It is important to make this your focus at the beginning of each day to set your attention on that which you want rather than on that which you do not want. This can be challenging to do when you are personally in the midst of your own personal travails that need your attention in each moment, but you will find that this practice serves you well, for it sets the tone for your day and helps to keep you inspired and motivated to continue in this mindset for the rest of your day.

This is a testing time for all upon the Earth, there is much going on beneath the surface of everything that appears. All that one can do is honor the process and work your way through it.

This is a testing time for all upon the Earth, there is much going on beneath the surface of everything that appears and all that one can do is honor the process and work your way through it. There is a Light at the end of the tunnel, Beloved Ones, so rest assured that you are firmly on your path of Light and service and that you will continue to make inroads in establishing the Light of God that never fails by anchoring it firmly into the great crystal at the core of Mother Earth. All is as it should be and once the lesson is learned, (and this could happen quickly), it is time to move on into the next level. Continue to practice being the Creator of all that is before you. You are Masters in training and remembrance and will remain so until your personal breakthrough occurs. At some point in the not too distant future, you will experience a personal revelation that will move you upward and forward through the next steps.

Remember that all is a choice and that you will expand your boundaries in your own unique way. We from the higher realms are always with you and continue to offer the greatest Light and love that has ever been experienced by any of you. We love and serve each of you and honor the Light that you are.

There is always a higher perspective to any situation.

There are many conflicting energies impacting you and it is a time to work diligently to maintain balance and equilibrium. You will need to practice grounding into the Earth first thing each morning and perhaps more often throughout your day. Spend as much time in nature as is possible for you; it is helpful to just relax and allow yourself to just be, without thinking or analyzing. For many of you, the mind has been working overtime and you have been having trouble falling asleep. These are challenging and perplexing times and great diligence is needed to stay in your integrity. As the energies increase, so does the pressure on your emotional and mental bodies. Be forgiving of yourselves and others and practice being an observer, watching your actions and reactions and try to learn from them, for there is much that can be learned about yourselves at this time.

The world as you know it is quickly changing and this will most definitely continue on in the times ahead. Always strive to look within yourselves when faced with trying situations and rise above them into the higher octaves for a different and calming perspective. There is always a higher perspective to any situation and it is very helpful to focus your energies in this way, for higher assistance is available to be tapped into. Even though you may feel alone at this time, remember that you never walk alone, that there are always your personal guides and angels working with you. We whisper words of love, comfort and upliftment to you. We tickle your funny bone to make you laugh out loud so that the heaviness of these old programs, patterns and energies that you are transmuting do not take over completely in your consciousness.

As you transmute the lower energies, the Earth is being lifted into a more peaceful place, even though what you see around you looks anything but peaceful; be assured that peace is making its appearance in your everyday affairs. Love and hope spring eternal within all hearts and these lower energies can be overcome through persistent effort. Holding a selenium crystal is very helpful for clearing unwanted energies, for these crystals are always clear, positive in their effects and deflect any heavier vibrations automatically and never have to be cleared. Placing your jewelry or sacred objects, your divination cards or any other items that you want cleared of unwanted energies on a selenium crystal slab will quickly clear their energy field.

Watch for wonderful synchronicities in your daily lives and practice feeling grateful for all the wonders around you, and for the beautiful beings who walk the human path with you in their journey into Oneness.

Watch for wonderful synchronicities in your daily lives and practice feeling grateful for all the wonders around you and for the beautiful beings who walk the human path with you in their journey into Oneness. More of your soul aspects are integrating within your greater energy field and this is a necessary process on your ascension journey at this time. Remember that you are beacons of Light and that you are here to shine that Light as you partake in the entire gamut of human experience and rise above it. This is what you have been training for, Beloved Hearts, and it is now becoming manifest all around you and within you. Be joy, be love, be happiness and feel gratitude for the opportunity that has been placed before you.

As each day goes by, know that you have successfully traversed the next step on your journey of ascension and that you are now filling your physical, mental, emotional, spiritual and etheric bodies with a greater

Light. As this occurs, your physical bodies and emotions, especially, are affected and this takes its toll upon your energy fields. When this happens, take time out to rest and be good to yourselves. Try to equalize your thought processes and keep them as neutral as possible, for the moment you engage in a thought of a lower vibration, it inexorably begins to draw your focus to these lower levels and the dramas taking place around you. Surround yourselves with the pure White Light often throughout the day and before bedtime, all it takes is stating the intention and it is done.

Love is the most powerful and mighty force in existence. Nothing can withstand its transformational abilities, for the heart, once touched by love, is forever transformed!

There is great import as more of the great crystals that have lain dormant for millennia become activated once again. There will be celestial alignments of great importance and significance, and greater energies, more potent and intense than ever before will begin to inundate the atmosphere of Earth and all her inhabitants. These powerful energies will bring great cleansing and will bring up personal and world karma which will surface in the lives of all. You, the Lightworkers, have already been prepared to be at the forefront of this movement and many of you are now ready to move into the next phase of integration with your Light body, your Divine essence.

This will be a very interesting and intense time for all upon the Earth and indeed, the Earth herself. Your Light and focused intentions each day, calling upon the higher forces of Light will aid greatly during the times ahead. As each person is touched by these great and powerful energies, it will initiate transformations at all levels and much depends upon the awareness level of each recipient of these energies, for the greater the awareness of what is occurring, the more equilibrium is maintained. Gather together in groups to pool your Light and energies and surround the atmosphere of Earth in a great circle of Light and send love into this field so that, by intention, it touches each and every heart upon the Earth.

These times that you are living in are the most challenging and most exhilarating humankind has ever experienced!

Love is the most powerful and mighty force in existence. Nothing can withstand its transformational abilities, for the heart, once touched by love, is forever transformed. It will be challenging for all of you, because once the energy of love touches every heart, all that does not resonate to this great power, begins to exit from your beings and you will be feeling anxiety, stress, tension and extreme tiredness in the coming days. Hold firm to your path and constantly remind yourselves that you are the Light and that you serve the Light. Sleep when the need overtakes you and listen to the promptings of your bodies. Drink plenty of water each day and find the time to sit or walk in nature, as this will help you ground these energies into the crystalline core and keep you and the Earth stabilized. Remember to call upon us, for we are ever ready to serve your needs.

These times that you are living in are the most challenging and most exhilarating humankind has ever experienced. These times are filled with the old structures and paradigms collapsing all around you and at the same time, the new way of living and being is being implemented. It is truly a wondrous time to be present in a physical body as these changes occur for you as an active participant in them. Well met, Beloved Ones! Many of you are leaving the old patterns behind you and embracing a new way, a way of sovereignty and personal power, a way of peace, loving kindness, compassion for all. How can it be otherwise, for when you gaze into the eyes of your sister or brother, you see their Divinity reflected there.

There will continue to be great changes taking place within the minds and hearts of humanity and great revelations will be taking place in each one's consciousness and understanding. Much will change as this happens, for the force of love is at work and there is no greater power in existence. Many things that were hidden will come to Light and the minds of humanity will be experiencing shock and awe as they become revealed. Know that you are prepared to take your places as this happens and that you have been placed in exactly the right spot to be of the greatest benefit to the Earth and all her inhabitants. Your Light is a shining beacon and you hold a greater role in the Divine Plan than you can imagine at this time. Your Light transmutes, transforms and stabilizes everything within the radius of your home for hundreds of miles around you. That is how powerful you are!

You have been placed in exactly the right spot to be of the greatest benefit to the Earth and all her inhabitants.

Go through these times remembering the Light that you are and daily affirm that you are the Light and the Light is needed now. As the cosmic forces pour down upon the atmosphere of the Earth, all will be affected in a way that is in keeping with the Path that each has chosen to walk in these changing times. Let go of the fetters, the illusions and the games that are still playing around you. We understand that this is very difficult to do when it is your own loved ones who are in the midst of these, but you must hold steady your Light and your great faith in the Light of God that never fails, and never falter on your path. Call upon the forces of Light that surround you and believe that all is as it should be.

Each day, take the time to affirm the life that you envision for yourselves and your loved ones and hold steady to the vision. In the midst of the chaos, your visions will see you through. You are our front line teams; you are the ones who have held the Light steady upon the

Earth, even when you have been severely tested. We know that you have been and that it does not seem fair, that those who are so good, so kind, so loving are asked to bear such great burdens. Keep in mind that this too, shall pass and you will all see the Light of a new day upon your planet. Life as you have known it shall be forever changed for the better and all that you have so earnestly desired within your hearts shall come to pass. You will come to understand that not all is as it seems and the greater picture of your current experiences will begin to come into your awareness.

You hold the greatest love the world has ever seen within your beings!

The most important thing to remember is that you are loved beyond measure by we of the higher realms and that you are literally, never alone. Write down affirmations that empower you and repeat them constantly. Hold to the feelings of joy, anticipation and well-being, of excited anticipation for the new era that will soon come to pass. You can do this, Beloved Hearts, you can and will do this because you hold the greatest love the world has ever seen within your beings. As you remember who and what you are, the blessings you bring to those around you will become apparent. No longer will you be the invisible ones because of the Light you have held. It was necessary in order to protect you all and everything that you have had to live and endure was for a greater purpose. You are now in the home stretch of your journey and soon many more of your sisters and brothers will awaken and join you in this Great Work, and perhaps even your beloved family members will be amongst them. Take heart and keep on keeping on!

I would speak with you about the work you are all doing and how proud and honored we of the higher realms are to be in association with you. You are going above and beyond the call of duty and taking upon yourselves much that does not rightfully belong to you. You are bearing the weight of the burdens of your sisters and brothers in order to lighten

179

the load in their individual lives and in the overall consciousness of humanity everywhere upon the Earth.

Know, Dear Ones, that we stand with you in these endeavors and that you are never alone, even though it sometimes feels as though you walk through the valley of the shadows all by yourself. We are always with you, giving you strength and courage to face another day and endure through these initiations into the greater Light, for by the burdens that you bear, you are lifting the entire atmosphere of Earth into the greater Light. This will become evident as the changes continue to take place during the great and powerful downpouring of the cosmic rays now streaming forth upon the Earth.

It is you who has the capacity to endure the higher vibrations and frequency of these rays of Light in order to transduce, transform and step down these energies.

These powerful cosmic rays are meant to cleanse and purify everything they touch and there is much that still needs to be cleansed and purified, as you well know. Keep on keeping on, Beloved Ones, for it is you who are the great transducers of these energies, it is you who has the capacity to endure the higher vibrations and frequency of these rays and Light to transduce, transform and step down these energies so that those who are just awakening or about to awaken can withstand the intensity.

Can you see now how the work you are doing is of such vast importance? We see how mightily you suffer as you take on the karma of the world and bring it to Light. This is the reason you are here, Beloveds, to bring greater Light to the world and you are succeeding in this endeavor. Keep affirming and decreeing each day, for this helps you to stay focused and consistent in your efforts. Please know that practice makes perfect as you become master alchemists in creating the world of your highest vision.

All in the universe hold their breath in delighted admiration and anticipation as you align the energies of your beloved planet to the Great Central Sun as we all move forward to the higher dimensions of expression. You are honored and loved as we see that your individual Light grows increasingly stronger and brighter each day. Your physical bodies are becoming less dense and therefore can contain more of the Light that you truly are. This is a great blessing to all around you. As you continue to do this, your radius increases in ever increasing waves of Light and frequency and will connect as a great grid of Light, a great circle of Light and it is then that the Earth Star shall be born.

All in the universe hold their breath in delighted admiration and anticipation!

We salute each and every one of you, most Beloved of our Hearts, for your unswerving dedication no matter what transpires in your personal lives. You are truly becoming multi-dimensional beings and performing multi-tasks that most of you are not even aware of, but rest assured your Divine selves are greatly and intensely involved in every aspect of this work.

As you look around you, the world as you have known it is rapidly changing. All that once seemed solid is now in the process of dissolution and transformation. This is bringing many of you great sadness and pain but also great growth in spiritual perception along with a total re-evaluation of your purpose here on Earth.

Grieve not, Beloved Hearts, for as the dissolution comes, there is also great potential for growth and transformation that is taking place within the hearts, minds and souls of those who are giving you such difficulties at this time. All is as it should be from the higher perspective. We say to you, do not give up on your relationships with those whom you love, for all is not yet lost.

Your beloved ones need giant wake up calls at this juncture and you have agreed to accept the roles that you are now playing. What is playing out in your lives and relationships has required you to experience a 'dark night of the soul' and, as Lightworkers, you are helping them to open up to their higher potential. To you it seems as though all is lost and never 'the twain' shall meet, yet you will find that down the road you are each traveling, there will occur great transformations within your loved ones. As these transformations begin to take place, a greater realization of your value and worth to them will begin to take place within them. They will realize how blessed they have been with your presence in their lives and there will be opportunities for reconciliation.

Go within as often as you are able and spend as much time in nature as possible, for this will help keep you grounded and will soothe your soul.

What is needed now for those of you going through these experiences is to love and nurture yourselves. Go within as often as you are able and spend as much time in nature as possible, for this will help keep you grounded and will soothe your soul. Allow your loved ones to go through their process and try and detach yourselves from any expectations. Sometimes a temporary time away will create greater clarity within your minds and hearts and bring your situations into greater focus and you will get a sense of your next step and your way will become clearer.

As this happens, be open to receiving guidance and the synchronicities as they occur in your daily lives, for your personal guides and angels will do everything they can to give assistance. We are ever ready and will answer your calls with alacrity. Speak your truth and do not be afraid, for all will work out in a way that will leave you gasping with incredible joy. It will require greater patience on your part, for you must allow the time for this to manifest. You may have to spend this time removed from the situation, in order for order and harmony to be restored. Have faith and hold onto the love that you hold in your hearts, for the love is the answer in every situation.

Many of you are feeling the heaviness that you have been experiencing now lifting from you and you are able to feel joy, happiness and well-being once again. Now that you have valiantly been willing to experience your core fears and issues, it is time to let go and move on. There is much that is waiting for you to discover - all your innate talents and abilities that have been lying in wait just beneath the surface of your thoughts. It is time to rededicate your selves to exploring your own uniqueness and majesty. You are mighty, powerful beings and it is time for you to reconnect with you and what you really are!

There is much that is waiting for you to discover - all your innate talents and abilities.

Every situation and issue that you are confronted with gives you a choice; to choose to delve right into the experience or to stand back, go within and discover the root of the problem or challenge and decide to take the high road. This can be difficult to do when those you love are involved but distancing yourselves from them can keep you detached from the drama that is manifesting around you. Stay centered within the core of your own being, having faith in your own abilities and intuition. You do know the answers and they are within you. Take the time to sit in meditation, or just spend quiet time out in nature and allow yourselves to feel whatever needs to express through you. This is very helpful in gaining a truer perspective of your situation.

Humanity as a whole is becoming more self aware and many people around the planet are questioning those in authority. They want more good in their lives than they believed they could attain before. As people begin this exploration of their innermost thoughts and feelings, they will make relevant choices that are more responsible and more cognizant of the effects of those choices on those around them. This will create transformations within the minds and hearts of all who go through this process and it is not an easy one, as you know. The most important thing to remember is that love is the answer in every situation or issue, for the bottom line is that love is all there is. Sometimes, what is the most necessary is the love and nurturing of self.

If you find yourselves being 'stuck' in a rut of negative thinking, identify these recurring thoughts and create a substitute to replace the negative with the positive.

Do practice focusing on what you want in your lives consistently each day, for this is what will help in its creation. Use your visualization skills to create mind movies that you can replay over and over again, all the while knowing that you are creating the life and circumstances of your own choosing. If you find yourselves being 'stuck' in a rut of negative thinking, identify these recurring thoughts and create a substitute to replace the negative with the positive until it comes naturally to you. Be sure to involve your emotions in the process, for it is the experience of the feelings of your desired outcome that will bring it to you more quickly and easily. Start with a small project and as you experience success with it, your confidence will grow until you become adept at the process of creative visualization.

You who have been in the trenches of the ascension process are accomplishing more than you can possibly know in your present moment. You have the Ascended Host at your disposal and we are only too glad to be of service. I know that this is something I have said to you many times before, but it is true. It is also true that you get so caught up in your earthly lives that you quite often forget to ask us. We remind you that we must have your request before we can step in to give greater assistance.

Many of you have begun to understand that you have chosen to take on certain roles that have been puzzling to you for a long time; these roles required that you act in certain ways that were totally foreign to your previous way of living, thinking, acting and being. These roles were for a specific purpose, which was to overcome the illusions that humankind has been experiencing for millennia, in order to facilitate an easier time of it for your sisters and brothers who are now beginning to awaken to their truths.

> **The higher you rise into the dimensional realms, the more you live your lives in service for the highest and greatest good of all, for that is the highest expression of eternal love.**

You are beginning to enjoy these roles and are realizing that you have been going through initiations and are coming into the mastery of your human selves. This is so exciting to view from our perspective, for we have watched as you have born and experienced the entire gamut of human experience, and have emerged with your soul sparkling clean and ready for your new day. This will begin to manifest for those of you who are ready for next level. The fact that you went into your roles in complete and almost total blindness and had to fly by the seat of your pants says much about the greatness of your courage and character.

Not all of you have chosen to take on these roles, so if you feel confused by my words so far, then be assured that you have chosen another assignment that is equally important. You are volunteering almost constantly to use all of the tools of your multi-dimensional selves for the highest and greatest good of all and this is a sure sign that you are progressing into your world service. You are special and unique and you came here at this time of the great and momentous changes that are taking place to be of service to the Divine Plan for the Earth and all upon her. Many of you have been through this process many times before and are here at this time to be of assistance and to work upon your growth at higher and higher levels. As you know, the higher you rise into the dimensional realms, the more you live your lives in service for the highest and greatest good of all, for that is the highest expression of eternal love.

This service is a sure sign that the tasks you have chosen are leading to victory in the raising of the consciousness of humanity and all upon the Earth to ascension levels. This is a remarkable feat which is being accomplished in complete peace and relative harmony, even though it may not have felt that way as you have been going through the process. It is what you do in your galactic service to the Light of God that never fails. For you are galactic beings and have been in service not only in your human form upon the Earth but also on other multi-dimensional levels. Your work goes on continuously and it is done with joy, gratitude and a great level of humor and fun.

What a marvelous and majestic work of art your human form is, and still becoming! It adapts and adjusts to all manner of energies and frequencies and has the ability to travel up or down the vibratory levels almost at will.

There is much joy to find in expressing life in a human form, for there is a great infinity of experiences to feel and savor while manifesting in your human body. What a marvelous and majestic work of art your human form is, and still becoming! It adapts and adjusts to all manner of energies and frequencies and has the ability to travel up or down the vibratory levels almost at will. Many from our vantage point look upon this opportunity you are experiencing with some envy and great applause, for it takes great strength to withstand the lower energies that have been rampant in your world and still strive to overcome them to create a better world for all. You are to be commended for all that you have done and continue to do. We know and understand that it has not been easy for you, that it requires almost superhuman strength of will to not react to your situations in the typical human manner. That you strive always to bring equilibrium and balance as soon as possible while still coming from a place of love and compassion in your hearts.

186

In so doing, you are bringing your gifts of love to this world in a way that is harmonious, loving and kind, even though some of your personal experiences have felt anything but those qualities – nevertheless, on the higher levels of multi-dimensional realities, you knew what you were doing. Some of you have found that you played your roles most enjoyably and that you played them with zest until the novelty of that particular old emotion was thoroughly explored and transmuted into a higher energy form. This is in the final stages of completion for the majority of you who are reading this message. It is a time of completion and also of new beginnings that are filled with limitless possibilities and probabilities for you that you could only call wondrous.

Your intuition is always leading you upon the path you have set for yourselves.

Be gentle and kind with yourselves and others; feel joy and gratitude for the lessons these situations provided in all you have been experiencing. All is as it should be and in spite of the seeming chaos, all is in Divine Order. Know this, Beloved Ones, and keep on keeping on!

Many changes are now taking place within you and around you as the dimensions are beginning to come closer together and the veils that have kept you blind are being lifted from you. You will notice that your perceptions are getting ever more accurate and your intuition is always leading you upon the path you have set for yourselves. Look around you and notice how everything is feeling the oneness of all that is. Those of you who have been doing your inner work are beginning to feel a greater lightness of being and you are beginning to experience more moments of joy and bliss for no apparent reason other than it feels so good.

Our Scribe has now begun a steady thought stream of 'thank you' and is training herself to be in deep gratitude at all times. There has been and still is, many challenges in her daily life and in her beloved family members lives that have tested each. As in the lives of each of you, our Scribe has had to walk the ways of this world and experience the many challenges that beset humanity. Many seeming injustices have occurred without apparent purpose, and yet, she has been able to keep her bottom line – and that is – that love is the greatest force in the universe. You are also connecting deep within to the core of your being, and are emerging stronger and brighter than ever. We know it has not been easy, but it is necessary and there will come a time when all that has happened will be made totally clear to you.

- Chapter 12 -
Stepping Into Your Mastery

Have faith in your Divine self and trust that you are being guided to be in the right place at the right time, doing exactly the right thing. All is as it should be and the deeper purpose of many of these tests and trials will become apparent in retrospect, for this is the process of learning as it takes place upon the Earth. These changing times require you to be adaptable, flexible and able to change plans at a moment's notice. Also to be able to bend and move as the willow tree whilst at the same time embodying the qualities of the upright and mighty oak, whose roots go deep into Mother Earth. Cast your roots down into the center of Mother Earth and take some time each day to connect to her in whatever way works best for you. Feeling the oneness of all life is now the next step on your path to ascension.

You will begin to express yourselves in a greater capacity than ever before and your words will carry the essence of the greater being that you truly are. Do not sell yourselves short, Beloved Ones, for truly you are the Light upon this world. What you say, think and do has enormous impact upon the mass consciousness of this planet. When you find yourselves expressing thoughts, words and feelings that are not of the highest vibrations, realize that this is the cleansing process that is occurring and try to have a sense of humor about it, so that you have the ability to laugh at yourselves and to forgive yourselves for any seeming transgressions. Realize also that the more you decree the Light, the greater will be the resistance from those parts of yourselves that you have carried with you in this lifetime and other lifetimes as well, which are ready to be transmuted and brought into the Light. This is why it is important to persist in your daily disciplines, for daily practice makes this process become much easier.

Do not look so much at what is being expressed upon the world stage but tend to your own 'garden' to ensure an abundant harvest of all the good that you desire and deserve, for this is what will manifest, as surely as night follows day.

Do not look so much at what is being expressed upon the world stage but tend to your own 'garden' to ensure an abundant harvest of all the good that you desire and deserve, for this is what will manifest, as surely as night follows day. Always honor your selves and your needs and listen to what your body and your soul wishes to impart to you. This process is ongoing and does become easier and more filled with grace as you work through them. Love yourselves and be patient with one another. We are deeply grateful to be working with you during these exciting times that are even now having a far reaching effect upon everyone and everything upon your beloved planet Earth.

For many of you, there will now be a cessation of the situations that you have been trying to work your way through and there will be more feelings of lightness and joy in your daily existence. This, too, is part of your task at this present time. The world you live on is in great need of the feelings of joy, happiness and well-being to counteract and balance the general mood of the populace at this time. The more you can stay in these uplifted feelings, the greater the upliftment of the frequency of the mass consciousness field.

All is well and on track now. I speak to the beloved Lightworkers of the world who have toiled ceaselessly to overcome the temptations of their human egos that have been operating front and center within the situations in your daily lives, within your relationships, whether personal or work related. This is a time of trials and tests, a time of initiation, and we ask you to stand as a beacon of Light, love and peace in your very homes and neighborhoods, as this assists in bringing stability and balance to all.

The world you live on is in great need of the feelings of joy, happiness and well-being to counteract and balance the general mood of the populace at this time.

All is changing around you and standing firm in the core of what you are is of utmost importance at this time. Do not doubt yourselves when you are called to answer for the actions, thoughts and deeds of others within your circle; remember that you do not need to take on their challenges. You are in their lives to uphold the higher version of themselves. It is only through the facing of each challenge personally that growth and awakening will take place. Each situation must be experienced firsthand and no one else can walk their path for them. As they do this, they will gradually awaken to their greater potential.

You are to stay calm and radiate peace and love, to practice acceptance of what comes forth from those around you. As you grow more proficient in this, you will realize that you have been coming into your own mastery, and life will again take on the sense of great adventure and opportunity in these changing times. By your presence, you can transform situations and be pivotal in the influence of the Light in each situation that you find yourself in. Many around you will be purging long buried thoughts, feelings and emotions and you will have to remember not to take personally all that comes forth through them. It is not for you to take responsibility for these, you are just to observe and witness.

Your calm demeanor will have a steadying influence on those around you and your leadership will be sought. You will be in demand for your insights and your services and you will be hard put to maintain a balanced way of life, but this you must do, for the most important thing is to keep the stability and balance in the overall energy of those around you. Call upon the Ascended Host to give support and assistance when you see the need and remember that we are here to help, guide and support you. This is what we promised to do before you came here to the Earth. Your requests are heard and honored at all times.

The more you can stay in these uplifted feelings, the greater the upliftment of the frequency of the mass consciousness field.

Go beyond, Beloved Ones, and ask to experience more joy, more wonder, more magic, more feelings of inspiration and upliftment, for these will help to anchor the higher cosmic energies into the Earth's core. There is much that is waiting to bless and caress you – wonders that seem unimaginable at this juncture of Earth's, and your, transition into higher levels of consciousness. You are creating your new Earth reality and your creation is good, so hold steady.

There is much flux in terms of energy flow, with feelings of joy and happiness in the morning followed by moodiness, withdrawal or extreme sensitivity by evening. Try to anticipate this before it occurs by watching for cycles of occurrence, take note of this and be patient with yourselves and others, for the energies now coming in are re-aligning your energy fields in a way that will bring in more life force energy and this will be felt particularly in the lower chakra regions. Practicing deep breathing to bring balance is very beneficial at this time as well as the drinking of more water so that the energy can flow more harmoniously through you. If you feel the energy being 'stuck' in one particular chakra, getting out in nature and walking briskly will help to move this energy in a more balanced flow through all your chakras, revitalizing and empowering each one as the energy flows through you. Intending this to happen will make it so.

This is a testing time for all upon your planet and your bodies are being transformed at an incredible rate, if you could but see it. As it stands now, you only feel the various discomforts that occur within you, such as great heat waves that come suddenly so that you feel that you will combust if you do not cool yourself down in some manner. Most of you are steadily feeling the energy flowing through your feet and have noticed this flow is getting stronger each day. Remember to state your intention to serve as a transducer of the powerful energies that are coming in and that these energies ground into the core of Mother Earth. As you do this, you will begin to feel the pulsation of the Earth and become more attuned to what is happening within her. Many of you have been feeling this for some time now and have sent your energies to the core with the intent that it be used by Mother Earth wherever she needs it the most and in this way have averted many drastic Earth changes.

Practice being the Master of your life and destiny, begin to see and feel yourselves as the powerful beings you truly are and sense yourselves as being 'larger than life'!

You are becoming more strongly the co-creators of the world you live in and as you practice your disciplines, begin to voice your intentions firmly, authoritatively, to bring into manifestation that which you want, be it personal or in world service. Practice being the Master of your life and destiny, begin to see and feel yourselves as the powerful beings you truly are and sense yourselves as being 'larger than life'. Practice makes perfect and you will soon get the idea and begin to incorporate it into every facet of your life until you are the Master of your body and processes.

Do not forget that the most important element of this Mastery is the embodiment of your Divine self and walking again as a Christed One upon the Earth.

This requires purity within one's body, mind and motives and the focus must be within your heart. Picture a golden sun radiating its bright energy from your heart to everyone and everything around you. Beam a pink ray of Divine love to the heart area whenever you meet with another person, for this is the standard greeting elsewhere in the universe. This practice alone can create peace and harmony very quickly within all relationships upon the Earth. Simply beam love to the heart of the other when you first see them. If you can train yourselves to do this automatically, you will have done a great service to all. We ask that you continue to practice, practice, practice. You have everything you need within you and are now beginning to discover this.

Beam a pink ray of Divine love to the heart area whenever you meet with another person, for this is the standard greeting elsewhere in the universe.

Many of you are beginning to feel joy in your daily lives again. This is a sign that you have passed through the 'dark night of the soul' in whatever form it took as karma to be acknowledged, released, transmuted and cleared and are now coming into completion with this process of ascension. It means your test of faith was met with success and an initiation into a higher consciousness is now coming to pass.

You it is, who has volunteered to be here in this present moment, successfully navigating the cosmic currents and transducing those currents into the core of the Earth to be used for the highest and greatest good of all. As you ground and radiate this cosmic Light, the effects ripple outward from your being and make a deep impact upon the energy fields of others. These others then awaken to many truths and revelations that were available to them before which they did not understand or comprehend or even discern as important to them. This is now changing, Dear Ones, for the required number of souls who are awakened or are awakening has reached critical mass.

195

Things upon your world will begin to move much more quickly now and whereas before you felt as though you were walking in molasses and feeling stagnation, you will now find that events begin to transpire with a rapidity that might at times take your breath away. You are ready for the next step and this will become clear to you in your personal lives and you will begin to take action as you follow the dictates of your heart and your inner guidance. You will start manifesting much more easily that which you have been affirming and it may come so quickly that you may not recognize that it has manifested for you. We ask you all to be aware in the days ahead that your every thought, word, and deed has an impact upon your world.

We ask you all to be aware in the days ahead that your every thought, word, and deed has an impact upon your world.

This is why we have counseled you to create more peace, harmony and joy in your daily living and to connect with the elements of nature, for this is tremendously helpful in clearing your energies and holding your Light steady. When you sit quietly, and hear only the water lapping on the shores of a lake and listen to the seagulls or watch their antics come feeding time, you are connecting with All That Is and even if just for five minutes, this will restore your energy fields to optimum levels. It will become a more important practice for you to use and remember. Never forget that Creator manifests in and through nature and is not distorted but remains pure as the Source.

No matter what happens in your personal lives, realize that you have always had within you all that you need and desire, and all answers come more easily to you as you practice "being in the flow". Begin to discern your patterns and how they cycle in your interactions with others and how this affects the whole and begin to make those changes which will make you more the Master of your life. You are creating new patterns of being on every level and we of the higher realms draw closer to you each day. You are deeply and unconditionally loved and we ask that you extend this love by passing it forward.

Most of you have made great gains in terms of cleansing, clearing and releasing that which no longer serves you. There will still be some residual effects that will continue to surface from time to time, but overall, you have come through this period in leaps and bounds, in terms of soul growth and forward movement. There will be much activity taking place in the awakening of your sisters and brothers around you. Your work and your prayers that their Ascension process be easier and more filled with grace and ease than that which you have been experiencing, is in effect.

You are deeply and unconditionally loved and we ask that you extend this love by passing it forward!

What this means is their awakening comes with less shock and travail than was experienced by our beloved Lightworkers. There will still be those who have chosen to experience Earth changes for their greater spiritual unfoldment and this will take place according to universal law. It has been an interesting ride for you and some of what has been occurring still has some of you with giant question marks hanging above your heads. These questions will receive answers as you are ready to hear them. All is in Divine timing and for the highest good of all. There is much to 'tie up' as you complete your assignments and step into your Mastery.

Mastery entails the ability to adapt to whatever situations present themselves in your daily lives, for this is where you are of the greatest import. Life is to be lived and experienced first hand in order to transmute and transform that which still needs to be looked at, for it is through you that Creator moves. It is your hands, feet and physical being that Creator uses to implement the Divine Plan for the highest good of all. It is imperative that you understand that not all that has or is happening to you is because you have done something 'wrong'. Not so,

Beloved Ones! You are instruments of the Divine in the great unfolding of the Divine Plan for the Earth and you are much needed to bring balance at this time. Sometimes, there are words and deeds that you say and perform that have you puzzled and doubting yourselves as to the amount of Light quotient you hold. You are mirrors for each other, helping each other to see those parts of yourselves that need attention and awareness in order to facilitate the changes necessary so that you can all move forward.

You are instruments of the Divine in the great unfolding of the Divine Plan for the Earth!

It is a wondrous time to be on this planet. You are taking in more Light as you release all that no longer serves the Light. In this way, greater transformation of your physical, mental, emotional and etheric bodies is taking place. You are becoming more attuned to the energies and vibration of the Earth and many of you can hear this constantly now. There is a low bass sound that permeates life on Earth, a 'humming' that is apparent to those who are closely attuned to the Earth, such as yourselves, who have been serving in the capacity of transducers of cosmic energies.

This will become more important in times to come and will be a way to know and understand what is occurring around you, so if you have been questioning why you hear 'humming', know this is the reason and that you are blessed. In this 'humming' flows much information through the Earth's new crystalline grid, with a boost from the great crystals that have lain dormant for eons of time and that are now reactivated and brought online again in a unified and integrated way. Many of these crystals and their functions were shut down so that their energies could not be used again for destructive purposes and all is in place to insure that this never occur again.

The sense of 'time' itself is greatly accelerating so that you are now feeling as though you are not accomplishing all that you set out to do each day, which seems to have a much shorter span, or so it seems. The Earth is speeding to her new place in the universe and all seems to be moving accordingly. It is important to watch the animals and how they act, for these are the ways that one has, to learn to be 'in the flow' with the Earth and all that is transpiring. Attune to nature, and try to become more aware of the tree family, the bird family, the animal family and if you watch them carefully, you will begin to sense impending changes that are about to take place, As you practice this watching and observing, you will begin to pick up clues and hints intuitively of the happenings around you such as weather changes and even Earth changes.

Your perceptions are undergoing a radical change and this will become more noticeable as the transformation continues.

Know that you are proceeding on your chosen journey accompanied by the Company of Heaven. Be at peace and be your wonderful, kind, loving and generous selves, for this is who you really are. All of life can seem to be a risk but choosing love in all instances and situations will see you through.

Your perceptions are undergoing a radical change and this will become more noticeable as the transformation continues. Instead of fretting about how to meet your goals, just relax and go with the flow of what apparently is and stay connected with your inner core of being, for in this way, all the changes that are taking place around you will not affect your equilibrium as much.

The wheel of life continues its inexorable journey through the cosmos and you are privileged to be a part of it - all that is required is that you stay aware of your power to make choices that will empower you to be your own highest potential in manifestation. By your presence and your persistence to be the Light that you truly are, you are contributing to the highest and greatest good of all. All is well and as it

199

should be. You are the shining Lights and hope of the new world that is dawning and together we all create this wondrous happening. By focusing your consciousness on the present moment as often as you can, you are practicing mastery of yourselves and of life and the end result will be of great benefit to you and all around you.

The wheel of life continues its inexorable journey through the cosmos and you are privileged to be a part of it - all that is required is that you stay aware of your power to make choices that will empower you to be your own highest potential in manifestation.

We remind you to feed your physical bodies with foods of the highest vibration such as fresh fruit and vegetables and to drink plenty of clean water each day. Listen to what your body tells you it wants, even though it sometimes doesn't seem to be the right desire in your conscious awareness. Rest assured, your body elemental knows what it needs for perfect functioning and excellent health during these powerful times. If you are feeling great waves of heat within your body, it indicates a metamorphosis taking place in every atom and cell of your being, on all levels.

You are in the process of ascension, cleansing and purifying, in readiness to absorb the higher frequencies of the cosmic waves of energy that are now coming in. Take the time to be out in nature as often as is possible for you, as this will help to cleanse your auras and energy fields and keep them operating at the highest possible levels. Always connect and ground yourselves into the crystalline core of Mother Earth, especially if you find yourselves functioning too much in your mental body, with too many thoughts running through your mind.

The need to spend some time each day in a state of stillness by going within is almost a required practice in these changing times and will help you tremendously in attaining and maintaining balance.

Remember that most of you absorb the energies and thought forms of others around you, and that you need to be aware of this so that your daily walk upon the path you have chosen is more filled with grace and ease. By going within first thing in the morning and becoming clear in your own energy field, you will become aware when you go out in the world of those feelings and thoughts that come into your consciousness which do not resonate with your high intentions. These are most probably not your thoughts and feelings at all but someone else's. Ask us each morning to assist in cleansing your auric field of all thoughts, feelings and energies that are not in alignment with your highest and greatest good and then trust that you are receiving this assistance.

Much mental discipline is now required of you as you come into more of your personal power.

Much mental discipline is now required of you as you come into more of your personal power. As you do this, you become conscious co-creators of what manifests upon the Earth plane. The more you concentrate on creating a world of peace, love, harmony and joy, the more this will become manifest in your daily existence. Trust that your powerful intention to manifest the Golden Age upon this beautiful, evolving planet is coming to pass. Follow your inner guidance and dare to be the grand and majestic beings that you have always envisioned that you could be…in other words, DREAM BIG!

Many of you are making great progress in understanding the dynamics of the challenges you have been going through. Each situation has helped in your growth as a human being to expand your previous boundaries and you are ready to let more Light and joy into your daily existence. Look around you and breathe in the fresh air and enjoy the sun's rays upon your face. Imagine yourselves as a beautiful sunflower reaching up to the sun, unfolding its radiant petals and blossoming into joy. The work you have done is now ready for harvest. We advise that you take time to fully and completely throw yourselves into your decrees and affirmations, visualizing yourselves as the masters of your lives in all ways.

It has not been an easy path for most of you but you have stood your ground and kept your 'line in the sand', persevering in your belief and conviction that the power of love will prevail in all the situations that have been testing you. It has not been in vain, for not only has your personal growth and Light increased, but also the Light quotient upon the planet. Never underestimate the power that you bring for the highest good of all as you practice your daily disciplines. You are making a difference!

Follow your inner guidance and dare to be the grand and majestic beings that you have always envisioned that you could be.

As the Light quotient grows around the planet, so too, do the sleeping ones arouse themselves, look around them and start their seeking and questing for truth and answers to their most burning questions. They question the purpose of life upon Earth, who they really are and the purpose for their being here at this time. As events happen in their daily existence, they begin their journey into the Light and begin to face what you have already worked your way through as you persevered each day. You have been the pattern breakers and are now the pattern makers, blazing a trail for those who come next. By your work you have paved the way for these ones, and though they must do their own individual work, they have at their disposal, a wealth of knowledge and information to help them on their soul journey.

You are ready to hone your receptivity to bring in your Divine self into greater manifestation in your body elemental. The energies continue to assist you in this process. Be sure to continue the drinking of copious amounts of clean, pure water and taking time each day to be outdoors so that your auras and energetic fields are cleansed and strengthened. Be sure to rest when you feel tired and take care of yourselves, for this is a most auspicious time in the cosmic calendar to avail oneself of great progress. Remember that there is usually a price to pay as you ingest and assimilate greater energies into your being and that there will be a period of adjustment while your physical, mental, emotional and spiritual vehicles absorb more Light and integrate with all aspects of your being. Step by step, you are transforming and transcending all previous boundaries and belief systems. You are daily proving that the human family is made of wondrous stuff and that you have within yourselves the ability to create miracles in your lives and in your world.

Step by step, you are transforming and transcending all previous boundaries and belief systems.

Hold onto your high visions of the world you wish to live in and keep on, Beloveds, firm in your resolve to be the beacons of Light that you contracted for before you incarnated upon this beautiful planet Earth. Continue to put one foot in front of the other and you will, in good and Divine timing, find your Path before you paved with gold, a path that will open up limitless possibilities, bringing to you opportunity to transcend your former limitations and take your rightful place in the Garden of Eden that is even now beginning to manifest once again on Earth.

Hold firmly and strongly to these visions and stay the course, affirming often that which you desire in your personal life. Daily state that you are willing to change all that needs to be changed within yourselves to bring you into greater alignment with your Divine Self and the Universe will respond with everything you need to bring this into manifestation. Above all, love and honor yourselves and take the time often to give yourselves little rewards for a job well done. These small acts will bring more of the same into your world. It is time that you enjoyed the fruits of your labors. Remember that joy is not something that happens TO you, but is something created by you! You, alone, have that power and choice. BE IN JOY!

There has been a great many physical symptoms occurring within you as you adjust your fields to the higher energies. You will find yourselves experiencing great tiredness from the assimilation of these energies and it is then the time to rest as much as you can. Your physical bodies are experiencing many changes and giving your body rest when it requires rest will help greatly to bring you back to comfort.

The feeling of joy automatically increases your Light quotient and frequency level.

You are finding subtle or not so subtle changes, in the way people around you act towards you. It will seem as though they are seeing you for the first time. This is because the energy that you have been grounding into the Earth through your physical bodies has now expanded in a greater radius around you and it is affecting and increasing the Light quotient in the atmosphere of Earth and subsequently effecting a positive change in the people of the Earth.

Your loved ones will pour their attention upon you in an effort to connect and show you in many different, wonderful ways that you are important to them. What you will be seeing, Dear Ones, is good karma returning to you and it will no longer hold true that the "good girls and guys finish last", for your past efforts will now begin to bear fruit in whatever way most pleases, fulfills and brings you the greatest joy.

Feel the joy as it wells up within you and try to remember this emotion so that you can bring it up at will and use it to keep yourselves in this state as frequently as possible. The feeling of joy automatically increases your Light quotient and frequency level and this will help you in your anchoring of your Divine self for a greater and more conscious connection. This is the next level now and it will be uncomfortable for quite some time as adjustments and attunements are made for greater integration. Remember to ask each day for assistance in integrating your

Divine self energies with grace, ease, comfort and safety and your angelic teams will work unceasingly to help you to do this.

If you are finding yourselves with seemingly overwhelming symptoms, always remember to ask for assistance from your angelic team and then lie down until it passes. Your bodies are going through tremendous change, listen closely and eat when you feel hungry rather than when it is your established routine to do so. Above all, trust in this process and that what you are experiencing in the situations in your lives is for a higher purpose. Become aware of each moment, for this is the way to your Mastery. Follow your heart's promptings in whatever way it leads you even if it seems strange and lacking in common sense. Your heart knows what is necessary for greater progress in your expansion of self. Practice focusing on your high heart chakra several times a day until you can feel it pulsating with energy.

Keep on keeping on, Beloved Ones, there is much change on the road ahead and you are cutting the path for others to follow.

- Chapter 13 -
Securely On The Path

The sense of acceleration continues to be a significant factor in your daily lives. It is a time of doing your very best and allowing yourselves freedom from the stress of "should's and must do's". This requires the ability to go easy on yourselves in every way and to accept that you are in a human body and not only that, a human body that is in the process of great transformation and change and that you do have certain limitations because of this. Accept this for the time being and realize that all good things come to those who persevere. Your soul's goals are being accomplished whether you think so or not. Your soul operates in spherical time, not linear time and implacably continues the unfolding of your personal and universal Divine Plan according to Divine timing rather than human linear timing.

Be at peace, Beloved Ones, you are securely on the path that you have chosen for yourselves. You are doing your part as best you can, given your consciousness and comprehension of what is transpiring in your personal world (micro) and your greater world (macro). The trick at this time is to learn to focus on the moment you are in, with as much of your attention as is possible for you. This will help you to eventually attain Mastery of your life, for the more mindfulness you apply to each moment of your existence; the greater ease is created in your outward manifestations of your inner processes. Truly, we are in awe of the capacity you are showing in creating Mastery within yourselves.

The creativity you show in accomplishing this is marvelous to behold. You are well on your way to the completion of the issues you have long been grappling with. As with all those living upon the Earth plane, these events and situations aren't clearly visible until much later, when you review the events from a different perspective of hindsight. We must say, that from our perspective, you are much too hard on yourselves and we say to you, the only failure is in ceasing to try!

You are becoming more attuned to Creator's goodness and greatness and this can only manifest as an ever increasing flow of blessings in your personal lives!

No matter how your "dark night of the soul" has been manifesting in your everyday life, know that you are never given more than you can handle at any given time. It is also true, that for whom much has been given, much is required. What that means is that as you move up the ladder of ascension and Mastery of yourselves, and you conquer the temptations and the trials that have beset you, you gain in greater power and awareness. This power and awareness must then be used for ever greater and more enlightened purposes and not strictly for personal gain. The biblical saying, from Mark 8:36 "For what does it profit a man to gain the whole world and forfeit his soul?" You know this wisdom in your deepest self and you have lived by this precept for many, many lifetimes.

Look for the positive changes within yourselves and that which is manifested in your outer reality as these changes are now discernible. You will find that greater synchronicity and a flow of blessings become a constant in your lives. You are becoming more attuned to Creator's goodness and greatness and this can only manifest as an ever increasing flow of blessings in your personal lives.

Many opportunities may be presented for you to move beyond your seeming inertia and inability to do, for you are deep into the assimilation of the energies that have been pouring down upon the atmosphere of the Earth. Although many of you are becoming more acclimatized to the ingestion of these energies and the direct effects they have upon your four body system, there are always ways in which you are able to tell that you are in the thick of the process and two of the ways are listed above. When you feel this is happening to you, what is required is that you listen to the promptings of your body elemental and *rest*! As you are all well aware, these energies are increasing in intensity and power and it is well for you to allow yourselves to rest and to continue your process of releasing all that no longer serves the Light that you truly are.

You must work through the transmutation of all that has no place in this higher vision of yourselves.

From our perspective we see more of your Divine selves integrating with your four body system. This will be an ongoing process to allow a more graceful assimilation of the greater Light becoming manifest upon the Earth plane through your physical body. Each time you decree a higher vision for yourself, what first has to happen is the release of all that you are not in alignment with in your higher vision! This is how the higher energies can begin to assimilate into your body physical. When you find yourselves bewildered as to why, when you have diligently practiced the decrees, affirmations, and visualizations in order to bring into manifestation your higher vision, you experience instead soon afterwards, more of that within you that is not resonating with that higher vision.

Be assured that this is a gradual progression into a more refined version of yourselves, for in order to be a Christed One walking upon the face of the Earth, you must work through the transmutation of all that has no place in this higher vision of yourselves. No one else can do this work for you; however, you have a tremendous amount of spiritual help and assistance ever at your side should you decide to avail yourselves of this assistance. All you have to do is call upon your personal guides, angels and teachers to guide you throughout your day and then listen to the inner promptings to come through. Follow these promptings in trust that you are receiving the assistance you have requested. We also understand that when you are in the throes of the transmutation and the feelings of inertia that befall you, that it is very difficult for you to act upon even making the request for assistance. In this case, what is required is the resting of your physical, mental, emotional and spiritual bodies even if that means sleeping most of your time during the day and night. You will know when you have assimilated these energies by the return of greater energy and vitality within your being.

Understand that your Divine self cannot just come in suddenly and take over, for this would be a great shock to your body system and would negate all the effort that you have put in to achieve a higher vibratory frequency.

Know also that as you sleep, you are being "worked upon" by your spiritual assistants and you will most likely feel tweaks and twitches, fluttering and bodily sensations as this work progresses. We are trying to facilitate the changes that are occurring within your bodies in a way that is more comfortable for you. The word for you to ponder is PATIENCE, Dear Ones, with yourselves and with this process. You must understand that your Divine self cannot just come in suddenly and take over, for this would be a great shock to your body system and would negate all the effort that you have put in to achieve a higher vibratory frequency.

This process requires the understanding of the cycles that occur upon the activation of the greater energy outpouring from the cosmos. Also the willingness and intention to go through it no matter what – just hold the vision of yourselves becoming your Greater Selves, incorruptible and liberated from the influence of the lower energies that are running rampant through your worldly communication systems at this time.

As a fully realized human transformed into your Divine Presence, there will be no more stresses and concerns with the old ways of the business of life upon your world. All is changing, transforming and will relentlessly continue to do so in the months and years ahead until one day, your process will be in completion and you will walk the Earth manifesting a greater Light. As more of you go through your completions, your greater Light will add to the overall Light upon your planet and this will continue to assist in facilitating changes at the planetary ascension levels.

All over the world, the consciousness of humanity is rising to higher and higher octaves and this is creating change in a peaceful manner.

There is a great feeling of excitement and anticipation being felt at our dimensional levels which is coming from the Earth plane each time you take part in the momentous massive worldwide meditations. Truly, the energies are high! How wonderful it is to see people of all faiths from all over the world get together in common purpose to bring about a positive and lasting change upon the Earth. We applaud you for the efforts that are being made and for taking action at the time of these events. Your Light radiates outwards in ever greater and greater radiating circles of loving energy.

Many are now awakening to the realization that there is more to life than the continuous and relentless distractions that keep them ever chained to the same old scenarios, day after day. They are realizing that they have the power to change their world by becoming more conscious of their thoughts, words, deeds and actions. All over the world, the consciousness of humanity is rising to higher and higher octaves and this is creating change in a peaceful manner.

You are now fully cognizant that there has been a great purging taking place within all aspects of your physical, emotional, mental and spiritual bodies and that this is a requirement in order for you to keep climbing the ladder of your ascension into greater Light and consciousness. We see you so valiantly proclaiming the Light that you are and your intention to manifest your Divine self within you and through you, even when you have just finished releasing all that is not in alignment with it. This is good, for it means that you understand the need for self forgiveness as you release these old energies from every cell. As you do this, remember to invocate and ask for more Light to come in and replace what has just been released with the pure white light of the Christ.

The denseness is falling away as you lift yourselves higher and higher into the octaves of joy, peace, harmony, wisdom and aliveness!

It is time to relax into the knowledge that you are a Being of Light and that you are firmly on the path of restoring your innocence, your goodness and greatness. Much of what you are releasing has been planted within the cells of your bodies by the constant barrage of thoughts, words and images that have been influencing you through your television shows and the movies that you watch until it has become acceptable to speak to one another using low vibration words. As you continue to uplift yourselves, these will fall away from you easily and will no longer affect you or those around you with lower vibrations. The denseness is falling away as you lift yourselves higher and higher into the octaves of joy, peace, harmony, wisdom and aliveness.

As this occurs within you, you will experience longer periods of the feelings of lightness, joy and good will towards those around you. This state of being will ignite in those with whom you come in contact and

211

they in turn, will ignite others. This is what a Peace Ambassador does by just being who they really are without any of the masks that they used to wear in order to protect and shield themselves and their vulnerable hearts. It is now time to blaze these wonderful hearts and the Light that they radiate out to all around you! Radiate your Light, for more than any other time in the history of your planet, it is what is most needed in order to bring stability and order to the chaos around you. The chaos only means that the Light comes. It only means that all that does not align with the Light must fall away.

What a joyful time this is! Live, laugh, and love, you most wonderful and amazing Beings of Light!

Continue your decrees, visualizations, and meditations each day, and join together in Oneness when you can. This activity helps you to remain grounded and fully experiencing life in your physical body. What a joyful time this is! Live, laugh, and love, you most wonderful and amazing Beings of Light!

Many of you find yourselves 'processing' the latest influx of cosmic energies in a very introspective way and are feeling that you are in two or more places at once. This is your multi-dimensional self kicking in. You will be experiencing yourselves as this more expanded being to a greater degree from now on. Right at this moment in time, what is required is stillness and going within. It is a time of grace and relaxation in the art of being, rather than doing, a time for reflection and evaluation of where you have been, and where you see yourself heading in the future.

Life upon your planet is becoming more filled with Light and it is beginning to have an effect on humanity in general. Although there will continue to be much change and chaos, there is also emerging, a feeling of peace and harmony with all of life. There is a oneness of being that is a profound statement to the successful integration of the energy downloads sent lovingly from the Creator. These energies assist all

212

upon the Earth to begin the process of refinement into greater Light expression and expansion. You are doing it, you are beginning to manifest your luminosity of spirit in your daily lives. Become more aware of the new you in the days ahead, all it requires is your awareness that this is so. Be the calm observer of the being who now walks your daily walk, feeling more passion and compassion for all that is so beautiful and precious on your world.

You are a shining beacon in the sea of darkness that is even now fading into the Light of the new dawn!

We of the higher realms continue to walk with you, we are ever at your side, giving counsel when asked and finding ways to make our presence known and felt. The veils between the dimensions are growing ever thinner and some of you are seeing things with your physical eyes that you never noticed before. Again, this is a sign that you are beginning to operate in your multi-dimensional bodies of Light and this will become more pronounced as more attention is paid to it. Continue to affirm and decree that your Divine self daily surround you with a great pillar of Light, a tube of Light that contains the Ascended Master substance to help you anchor this into your outer (physical) self.

As you daily repeat the invocation, you are assisting your physical vehicle to transform into its Divine expression. Many of you can feel the power of the energies that come through your crown chakra. As you invoke, this sensation is a sure indication that your Divine self is reaching down to anchor more of its Divine Essence into your heart chakra and solar plexus. It is manifesting within you as your more unlimited and greater expression of your Divine self. We guide our scribe to the invocations that best assist you in moving to the next level of your spiritual journey through the monthly decree page.

We thank and honor you for the work that you are doing with great persistence and firm faith, knowing that by invoking Light and intending it, it is brought into your lives. You are a shining beacon in the sea of darkness that is even now fading into the light of the new dawn.

As the cleansing and healing continues to take place within your hearts, an expansive feeling begins to take over, a feeling of hope, peace, joy and happiness. Savor these moments, Dearest Hearts, for in these moments, you have raised the frequency field around your dear planet Earth. Each moment spent in joy is a moment for magic to occur; each moment spent in laughter is a moment for miracles to happen. Each moment is All That Is in the here and now. See yourself savoring the moment. If you are walking, know that this is where you are in this moment – walking. If you are washing your windows, feel yourself completely in that moment. Start to focus your attention always in the here and now. As you do this, you will find that you are in the consciousness of your greater self experiencing self as you!

Being in your body is a miracle in itself. It is a privilege, an honor and a great adventure!

As you practice this discipline each day, you will discover your inner power and this will enable you to accomplish miracles in your life. Being in your body is a miracle in itself. It is a privilege, an honor and a great adventure! Become aware of the miracle that is you, observe your actions and if you do not like something in your life, change it! There are always new ways of viewing each situation, new and uplifting solutions that can overcome and wash away old issues and patterns just by giving these new ideas a chance to enter your consciousness and take root. This is the way to mastery of your being, to come into your full power as a loving, enlightened Divine being of Light. By spreading your good thoughts and feelings everywhere you move, living each moment as the love that you embody and truly are, you let your luminosity from within shine forth!

Have you ever wondered why you are experiencing the feeling of darkness? It is because you need to recognize your feelings of lightness, to know beyond a shadow of doubt that you are Light. No matter what difficulties you are experiencing, you are of the Light and you are never alone. By allowing love to enter your heart, it will transform the moment. Make love your bottom line, Beloveds! If there is something or someone that you cannot trust completely and it makes you feel unsure, take the risk and just love and allow. In the moment that you do this, a transformation takes place within you and in your situation and the world around you is changed. Your personal world and the events in it do not happen by accident. It is all brought about by your thought processes and of course, the over lighting of your Divine self for the greater purpose of soul expansion and consciousness. It is in your greatest challenges and experience of frictions in your life that the mastery of self is honed and takes place.

It is in your greatest challenges and experience of frictions in your life that the mastery of self is honed and takes place.

You are learning once again, the mastery of self whilst in a physical body. You are an alchemist turning lead into gold. You are the gold, Beloved Ones, and worth every effort you have ever made to bring this into being. You are the golden children of Creator. The golden Light of the Christ Consciousness flows through every cell and atom of your being, through every chakra and power center, every pore of your skin. Take this thought and build upon it each day for you are THAT. Love yourselves unconditionally and practice manifesting through your being each day the nine fruits of the Spirit; love, joy, peace, patience, kindness, goodness, trustfulness, gentleness, and self-control. This is truly the road to Mastery.

You have been deep into introspection lately and are evaluating all that has occurred in your life to this point. It was a time of becoming aware of and letting go of all patterns that have been subconsciously present in your cells for a very long time, sometimes for many lifetimes.

This cleansing is very necessary and can be likened to taking a sponge, soaking up all that was spilled and then wringing it out under running water until the water runs clean. In this case, the 'water' is prana or life force. All that has hindered the easy and natural flow of prana through your body system is being "worked upon". Each time you intend and decree Light, what surfaces from the deepest levels of your being is all that is not Light until it is completely cleansed from your system. It is uncomfortable for you, we know, because you assumed that you had already been through this process in your previous years of growth into your life as a way shower. You may feel that you should have already been ready to take on the greater Light of your Lightbody.

You are an alchemist turning lead into gold!

Your Lightbody is anchoring within you in as comfortable a way as is possible and sometimes it does not feel comfortable. Nevertheless, know that progress is being made and that your cells are renewing themselves and holding more Light now. Our advice is to let go the ego and sit in surrender to your Divine self in utter simplicity and openness, love, trust and humility and just be still. Many times you suffer because you feel you must be doing something actively in order to fulfill your own growth and potential and become frustrated when it does not happen.

This is the time for surrender, peace and calm, staying in a state of waiting, incubation if you will, while a metamorphosis takes place within you. Honoring the signals of your physical, mental and emotional body is very important at this time. If your body feels tired all of a sudden, listen and take time to lie down and rest. If you suddenly feel enormously thirsty, take the time right then to drink at least two glasses of water, blessing the water that you take into your body. Remember, you are now becoming conscious alchemists and learning to become very aware of self in every moment.

The mastery of this process will help you make leaps and bounds in your spiritual journey. This is the way to understand yourself as the spiritual being embodying your body elemental for the purpose of experiencing itself in you and through you as you. Learning to see the beauty and wonder in every thing around you is a big step forward on your path. Everything upon the Earth is unique and incredible in itself, every little thing. Even the tiniest little cell in your body is a fully conscious entity and just loves to be acknowledged as such. Everything works in unison to provide a form that is healthy, whole and perfectly functioning so that your Divine self can experience the here and now.

Greater integration is now taking place on all levels of your being, not just the physical.

Some of you are beginning to ask questions out loud and then answering yourselves. This is a conversation that is actually taking place with your Divine self and we encourage you to continue in this practice, for it creates an open connection for the free flow of insight, guidance and direction for you each day. We do understand that talking to yourself while walking along an aisle at Wal-Mart might cause some curious looks from others around you! In this case, do it more discretely but do it, Dear Ones, for greater integration is now taking place on all levels of your being, not just the physical.

We continue to assist when called upon to do so and literally stand beside you each day waiting for your call. Your growth to the next level is very important to the overall plan in raising the Light quotient upon your planet. Whatever difficulty you may have found yourself in, tune in with us and ask for assistance. We cannot live your life for you, but we most certainly can guide you onto the path of least resistance and greater integration. It bears repeating often, Beloved Hearts; that you are loved beyond measure and are treasured deeply by your Family of Light.

You are making great gains and headway even though you may not be seeing this manifest in your daily life as yet. Be assured that this is

217

taking place and your ascension process continues unabated. The cosmic energies being beamed to the Earth and everything and everyone upon her continues relentlessly and all is being cleansed, healed and recalibrated to wholeness and the perfection of their original divine blueprint. This will continue, Beloved Ones, and believe it or not, it will become easier for you, simply because you have persisted in your disciplines and in your determination to be the highest and best that you can be.

You will soon feel a lightness of being and the feelings of joy will be your daily companion as you walk your spiritual journey into the adventure of a thousand lifetimes!

Your sisters and brothers around you will find it somewhat more difficult as they awaken further but the path of Light and purification that you have cut, that you have blazed, goes before them and makes easier their way than it might have been. Truly you are mighty warriors of Light and you are the mighty forces of the greatest power in the Universe and that power is love. Take time to just BE and enjoy the energies, the peace and goodwill that abounds during this time. It is a time of the joyful celebration of the greater Light coming more fully back onto the Earth and into the hearts of all of humanity.

Trust the guidance and the intuitive impulses that come to you. Know that you are divinely guided to walk your path in the highest integrity and moral standard. This will become the moral signpost in the days to come, for no matter how much you have been tested, your deep and abiding love for the Creator and the Divine Plan for the Earth has always been your driving force and motivation. You will soon feel a lightness of being and the feelings of joy will be your daily companion as you walk your spiritual journey into the adventure of a thousand lifetimes! The Universe is watching with wonder and awe at the glory that is now unfolding, and will continue unfolding in the years ahead.

Hold your heads high, Beloved Ones, you have stood your ground in your Light and highest integrity. You have loved all the dysfunctions that you found within yourselves back into the wholeness of the unified field of your higher being. Your Light is shining brighter and brighter and you are all easily discerned and seen by we of the higher realms and we add to that Light continuously. As you grow in your Light, awareness and love quotient, so too, does the influence of this spread outward in all directions to affect all within your sphere of influence. This sphere of influence that you wield is covering a larger territory now and it behooves each of you to visualize yourselves radiating your Light in a concentric circle from your home in a thousand mile radius around it. Take this to heart and consciousness, Dear Ones. You are powerful beyond your knowing at the present time.

You have loved all the dysfunctions that you found within yourselves back into the wholeness of the unified field of your higher being.

Continue to walk in your Light each day, speak your truth in your quiet and loving way. The more truth that comes from within every heart and soul upon the planet, the greater Light can come in. There are mighty events taking place in these times. Gathering together in unity and purpose will accomplish ever greater miracles. We are with you always.

The energy that is pouring upon the planet has been increasing in its intensity and greater diligence is needed to be at one with it. More time is needed for each of you to be in stillness or deep meditation. Try to find alone time each day, even if for just five or ten minutes. It is a time of competing energies that are swirling all around you and being in tune with your Divine Self is most helpful during this time.

We remind you that this is a most magical time, there is wonder and magic that abounds if you but look for it. It requires first of all, a change in your thinking by opening yourselves up to the possibility of joyous

219

occurrences. The universe is surrounding you with endless possibilities and opportunities and you have but to catch a falling star! This is a time of wondrous happenings and it all begins within you! Every day there is something wonderful just waiting to happen and you have but to be open to it. Start recording all these wonderful moments in a journal so that you can review them on a monthly basis and see how often they really *do* occur in your life.

This is a time of wondrous happenings and it all begins within you!

This is also a time to become aware of your thoughts as they occur in your thinking processes and just be an observer of them rather than becoming engaged. By being detached from outcomes you will find the enjoyment of life itself increasing. You are here not only to help increase the Light quotient and frequency of the planet but also to realize that you have been gifted life in a physical body and this is an awesome opportunity to explore what that means to you.

Send your beams of loving Creator energy to all of your loved ones and everyone you come in contact with. See yourselves as a being of golden liquid Light sending spirals of liquid golden energy to everyone around you. Send out your feelings of peace and good will and let the joy of this time seep into the core of your Being. Peace begins within you, Beloveds, and in turn, empowers you with confidence in your own uniqueness, talents and abilities.

Remember in the days to follow that you are ambassadors of the Creator and your way is the way of the pattern makers, the leaders, the way showers. The ones you have been waiting for are here NOW and they are YOU! You are THAT wonderful, Beloveds! By your thoughts, words and deeds, you can change your world. A Divine Alchemist is one who changes their world by their thinking processes and intends only the highest outcomes for all.

Remember to ground yourselves daily by visualizing the energy of the Great Central Sun coming down through your crown chakra, flowing through your spine, your legs, the soles of your feet and into the Great Crystal in the central core of the Earth, anchoring through the Great Crystal and returning the energy of Mother Earth up through the soles of your feet and back up through your crown chakra into the Great Central Sun in a continuous infinity loop. Love is all around you and within you. Celebrate it by being it!

Love is all around you and within you. Celebrate it by being it!

We applaud you for persevering through the most trying tests of faith and trust, in holding on to all that you have worked for and believed in. Truly, this has been a time of changes and transformations for all upon the planet and most especially for, the Beloved Lightworkers around the world. We thank you for holding the Light steady and for the anchoring of the greater Light through you, into the crystalline core of the Earth. This work has enabled a great leap forward for all upon the planet.

As you look around you in the coming days, you will see evidence of the value of the sacrifices you have made when you see your sisters and brothers awaken to the Greater life and begin to set their feet firmly upon the paths that you have cut for them. These paths are shining with pure Light and those who come after you will widen these paths so that the multitudes can know which way to go. Those who follow you will hold their vision high and will take the action that is necessary to create the positive changes upon the old outworn systems of this world. The world as you have known it is being changed moment by moment and even we of the higher realms hold our breath with joyous anticipation.

That which has been holding you back will fade and seem to be far in the distance. The way before you, the way showers of the world, will lead more definitively in the direction of the integration of the higher aspects of yourselves. You have been valiantly releasing and transmuting the lead that has been dormant within you into the gold of your higher authentic selves and this will translate into a greater freedom to walk this world in your true God given power and authority. Now it will be the task of the Creators that you are, to weave the filaments of your being into an incredible field of Light that will literally effect peaceful changes upon the Earth and within every heart that beats in rhythm with the heartbeat of Mother Earth.

Your lives have taken on greater transparency as you have striven to walk your path in the highest honesty, integrity, truth and Light.

You will find yourselves more in tune with the energetic influx of the cosmic flow of rainbow rays upon this planet and what was once hidden and hard to discern will now become as an open book. Your lives have taken on greater transparency as you have striven to walk your path in the highest honesty, integrity, truth and Light. From your current perspective, it has been a great struggle to maintain balance and equilibrium during these testing times but you have all come through with flying colors! The path of ascension for all upon the planet has become a viable possibility and probability.

Each day that you walk your walk and be in the Earth in your multi-dimensional bodies is another milestone in the history of this planet. Many inroads have been made and these you are aware of in the higher dimensions in which you move and work at the same time as you live your daily lives here on Earth. The world is a better place because you are in it, Beloved Hearts, and all upon her are blessed because you have chosen to be here now. You have met every challenge with strength, faith and courage and these attributes will be put to use as events move this world forward in the times ahead.

Accept the love and grace that surrounds you as you daily move through the lessons, insights and perceptions while you continue to balance any remaining karma that you have chosen to bring to harmony in this lifetime. Keep on keeping on, Dear Ones and know that you are loved and supported through it all by your Family of Light from on high. We strive to lift you up so that you may in turn lift up humanity and help them rise in unison with the Earth as the ascension process continues. May peace prevail on Earth as it is in Heaven!

I AM Hilarion

If you have enjoyed this book, your honest review on Amazon.com would be greatly appreciated!

Coming Soon:

The Hilarion Connection©, Book Two

GLOSSARY OF TERMS

Angels of Light – Illumined and pure beings of Light who serve the will of the Divine and are spiritual and loving beings that are not bound by Earth's physical laws.

Ascended Masters – They are humanity's elder sisters and brothers who hold us constantly in the light of their higher vision helping us to grow and evolve. They have transcended and ascended the lower dimensions of life on Earth in the physical realm and now extend their assistance to all upon the Earth who have awoken to their true Divine nature and seek their guidance on the spiritual journey back to Source. To name a few: Buddha, Vishnu, Shiva, Babaji Nagaraj, Krishna, Mohammed, Jesus, St. Germain, Kuthumi, Hilarion, Mother Mary, Isis, Pallas Athena, Lady Portia, Quan Yin, El Morya, Djwal Khul.

Ascension – A dimensional shift into a higher consciousness through an alignment with ones soul purpose and divine essence which requires one to release all previous belief systems, thought processes and ways of being that would hinder such movement into a higher evolvement of the human species. One ascends by becoming lighter and lighter in the most literal sense as the denser aspects of ones chakra system is refined and purified through diligent effort and spiritually focused intention. To ascend means to realize that one is in reality, the Light of the world. This was the whole purpose of Christ's mission on Earth at the beginning of the Piscean Age, to show humanity The Way.

Auric Field – The auric field is a collection of electro-magnetic energies of varying densities that permeate through the physical body of a living person or other living being. These particles of energy are suspended around the healthy human body in an oval shaped field. This auric field surrounds the body approximately 2-3 feet on all sides and extends above the head and below the feet into the ground. These layers or bodies start with the physical body which is the tangible form, then comes the etheric body, emotional body, mental body, astral body, divine blueprint body, celestial body and causal body. These layers or bodies affect the whole person on every level of being, emotional, physical, mental, and spiritual, thus the importance of daily clearing of one's chakra system.

Awakening – A process that takes place within an individual that opens them to a new state of awareness that they are more than human and are in fact, a part of the Divine. This awakening usually catalyzes an individual to begin a spiritual quest into finding answers to their questions regarding the aspects of higher consciousness and its relationship to their own spiritual journey.

Aware – A state of awareness of a being that is aware of itself as more than they once perceived themselves to be.

Bardo – The realm of the afterlife is called the world of the bardo. The bardo is the period of the afterlife that lies in between two different incarnations.

Behooves – A duty or responsibility for someone to do something that is appropriate or suitable in a given situation.

Being of Light – A spiritually motivated Being that vibrates at such a high frequency that they are perceived as a bright ethereal Light.

Castes - A system of the segregation of people, each according to their natural talents, abilities and spiritual gifts. A hierarchical system based on one's profession. Different professions were graded at different levels and the amount of respect accorded to them varied according to the hierarchical scale.

Chakra – The centers of spiritual power in the human body, usually considered to be seven in number, which are the main ones. There are many other more subtle centers that open with the gradual awakening of one's awareness and evolvement into a higher consciousness.

Clarity – The perception of wisdom and the ability to see the soul in action in the physical world which allows one to see the world of physical matter for what it is—a learning and experiential environment.

Co-Creator with God   To co-create, one needs to align their soul's desires and passions with their higher purpose and spirit, thereby tapping into Source energy and the divine force of the universe through conscious intention, which facilitates the process of manifestation and co-creation.

Conduit – A person who allows higher cosmic energy to move through them into the centre of the Earth to bring in more Light from the cosmos or into a place where the ascended beings can communicate with them clearly.

Cosmic Christ – A perfected Being who has aligned their human will to the will of the Divine within them. One who is virtuous and lives a good and noble life.

Cosmic Energies – Everything in the universe and beyond is made up of energy, the universal force. One can constantly and instantly recharge from an unlimited supply of cosmic energy through concentration and the use of their will by visualizing energy coming from the outer cosmic source through the medulla oblongata (see Glossary below for description) to any body part or into the Earth.

Crystalline Core of Mother Earth – Scientists discovered in 1995 with a sophisticated computer model of Earth's inner core that there is a giant crystal buried deep within the Earth at the very center, more than 3,000 miles down. This discovery has created a new science, the study of which is now ongoing.

Decreeing – As a child of the Divine, one has the power and the authority to speak out a creation or ideal in their life and expect to see it manifested in the reality of their world.

Descension – This process occurs when the four lower human bodies (physical, mental, emotional and spiritual) are purified enough to allow their Divine essence (who they are as a Soul) to manifest in and through them.

Divine Blueprint – Ones original Divine Blueprint is energy that is a pure form of crystal light which encompasses sound, symbols, sacred geometries, vibration, color, and a network of communication that knows only unconditional love.

Divine Dispensation - Is the ordering of events under divine authority as a special permission to not have to follow a rule or to

229

be bound by a particular code of behaviour or divine law in order to allow humanity to take advantage of the current opportunity to progress and evolve spiritually.

Divine Origins – Infers that there are powers or forces that are universal, or that transcend human capacities. Divinity always carries the virtues of goodness, beauty, beneficence, justice and other benevolent qualities which was originally the true state of being.

Divine Plan – Is the concept of God having a plan for the Earth and humanity and its ongoing evolution back to Source.

Divine Self – The Divine essence of one's being, the source of all light and life within them.

Etheric – Other dimensions above the physical - the astral, solar, etheric and causal dimensions which are somewhat similar to the physical plane, yet the higher one ascends, the more expansive, refined, lighter and less dense they become. These etheric states are becoming more discernable in the physical as the collective of humanity moves into a higher state of consciousness and awareness.

Family of Light – The Family of Light includes the Ascended Masters, the Archangels and the Angelic realms, the Star Nations and the incarnated volunteers who are on Earth to aid in planetary change and transformation. They are to bring in or 'remember' high levels of information, guidance and awareness and to anchor the energy of unconditional love. This is to aid in raising the overall energy of the planet. In this lifetime, each individual is to reclaim their spiritual power, ability and knowledge in order to use this knowledge for the highest good of all.

Third Dimension - Three-dimensional awareness has the basic qualities of time, space and matter. Physical awareness is three-dimensional.

Fourth Dimension – The fourth dimension is the bridge to other dimensions. It is the realm of ideas, the world of the imagination. In the fourth dimension, there is a pervading consciousness of eternity, where past, present and future simultaneously co-exist. Love is an expression of the fourth dimension as a shared awareness with all energy forms of the essential unity of all things.

Fifth Dimension – The fifth dimension is basically a change in the nature of time and space and how they are perceived. Ones consciousness becomes multi-dimensional in its functioning. This is the realm of ones light body reality. More information on a universal level is available for access and input. One needs to be open to rapid change and to remain open, fluid and flexible as this occurs.

Four Body System – This refers to the physical, mental, emotional and spiritual bodies of the human form.

Galactic Cycle – A galactic cycle is the duration of time required for the entire solar system to orbit once around the center of the Milky Way galaxy of which this planetary system is a part. It is also known as a cosmic year.

Golden Age – A golden age is a renaissance or revival of human civilization that is filled with great peace, prosperity and happiness and where human civilization makes great spiritual, artistic, creative, innovative and scientific progress.

Golden Rule – Is a code of conduct that asks people to treat others in a manner in which they themselves would like to be treated.

Great I AM Presence – Is the collective consciousness of all of ones lifetime experiences as soul aspects. Each individual has access to the incredible wisdom, knowledge and talents that are available to them through this eternal Divine Presence.

Heaven on Earth – Is a world in which life is lived in a state of peace, harmony, beauty, love, and goodwill towards all living beings where the Golden Rule is practiced as a natural expression of the human experience.

Higher Dimensions of Light – Is a state of being where one connects directly to the universal God through their inner divine essence and greater expanded Being.

Higher Self – Is the higher aspect of self that has learned all that is knowable within physical and multi-dimensional reality and possesses spiritual and human   knowledge, wisdom, and understanding which can be tapped into by each   individual who aspires to reconnect to this higher version of self.

Higher Vibratory Frequency – When one recognizes and accepts that they are a being of Light that is connected to Divine Source, their vibration lifts significantly as they practice to maintain this connection each day. Having a sense of self worth and confidence in oneself helps them to radiate high frequency light and energy.

Higher Realms – A state of pure undiluted consciousness and pure undiluted love.

Hilarion's Retreat – The retreat is in the etheric realms over the island of Crete where those who serve the flame of the Creators Divine Truth are taught the way of truth, and the revelations of truth. All sincere seekers are welcomed in this place of higher learning, one just needs to set the intention to visit during their sleep time.

Impeccability – A state of being and doing where one lives their life with unconditional love, gratitude, and respect for self and others in accordance with their highest truth, always honouring self in their integrity and soul direction.

Integrity – Speaking and acting honestly, always in the direction of the highest moral principals of truth and love and being true to ones higher vision of self.

Initiation – An initiation is an extension of one's consciousness towards an appreciation of universal realities. It was viewed by ancient philosophers as the greatest adventure and the greatest good that can be given to the human soul during their life experience on Earth. By ones enlightened action to overcome the domination of their outer senses through the perfecting of their inner spiritual faculties, they can come to perfection of self. Perfection of self is a personal accomplishment that is achieved by an individual through personal effort in practicing self discipline and self responsibility in all their thoughts, words and deeds. The great truths of life can only be given to those who have been tested in their personal character and understanding.

Karma – The sum of each individual soul actions in this and previous states of existence that decides their fate and destiny in future existences. All must be balanced according to Universal Law. That which is sowed is that which must be reaped.

Lady Gaia – Gaia is the personification of the Earth, the essence of the planet which is stored within the crystalline core of the Earth; a highly sentient Being who loves and cares for all of life upon and within the planet.

Light – The Divine Light of the subtlest frequency from which all creation has emerged. Light is a key attribute of Spirit. Light equals higher consciousness. This Light has creative intelligence, and purifies, heals and helps each individual in every way. This Light is Creator Source and is everywhere simultaneously and anyone can access this Light at any time through their intention and awareness.

Light quotient - Ones level of initiation on their personal spiritual path is measured in light or light quotient. Building light quotient means to anchor greater and greater frequencies of living light into ones cells.

Lightbody – The lightbody remains in, around and above the physical body but depending on the person's ego structure, it is not strongly felt and what is felt is distorted by the astral. A ground into the planet's core is necessary to pull in the lightbody by first raising the vibration of the astral body. Once the astral body has been cleared of all lower density crystallizations, the light body can shine through it and ground into the physical.

Lightworker – Lightworkers are individuals who have a great desire to help their world. No matter what else happens, it is a

Lightworkers greatest focus and passion to add more Light and positive energy to the world. In their hearts there is a connection to the Divine Source and an inner knowing of this Source as their Source. It is this connection that burns brightly within them no matter what happens in their outer circumstances. Anyone can become a Lightworker at any time they choose to live beyond only themselves.

Living Masters – Are highly evolved beings who have taken on human form on Earth over the ages bringing knowledge, wisdom & light to show humanity the way forward.

Mass Consciousness – Is the shared beliefs, ideas and moral attitudes which operate as a unifying force within society.

Masters – Ascended Masters belong to the Spiritual Family of Light that have guided and directed the evolution of life on Earth from the beginning of time.

Mastership – Having control over one's thoughts, emotions and actions in order to function at a higher level and frequency of consciousness. This is an essential requirement of each individual who aspires to greater consciousness and ability.

Medulla Oblongata – The medulla oblongata is a portion of the hindbrain that controls autonomic functions such as breathing, digestion, heart and blood vessel function, swallowing and sneezing. Motor and sensory neurons from the midbrain and forebrain travel through the medulla. As a part of the brainstem, medulla oblongata helps in the transferring of messages between various parts of the brain and the spinal cord.

Monad – The Monad is a conglomerate of the many souls that one is a part of. The Monad is a direct aspect of the force one knows of as God. Ones Monad supplies one with the life force, love and attention that one may need to maintain their existence and it is ones Monad that is ultimately responsible for ones evolution within the body of God.

Oneness – All life must work in harmony, balance, and respect for all other life. All life vibrates with feeling. And the natural state of feeling is love. We are all individualized reflections of the God Source. God is us and we are God. Each Divine self is in touch with every other Divine self. All unlimited souls resonate in harmony with each other.

Path of Light – Ones destined reality unfolds like a path of light before them as a direct consequence of ones aligning with and expressing their highest truth and intentions.

Planetary Ascension Levels – The Earth is ascending to a higher dimensional level of consciousness and humanity can join with the Earth on its ascension journey. This is a great cosmic opportunity for each individual currently incarnated on Earth to reconnect with their own Divine Essence and balance their individual karma in order to be freed from the requirement to reincarnate until all soul lessons are learned.

Portal – Is a doorway, gate or other entrance to a different reality than one is used to.

Prana – Practicing deep breathing exercises helps to bring in this life giving substance into one's body system.

Purification - Purification is a prerequisite for each individual on the spiritual path of enlightenment in order that they become totally clear and unencumbered to enable the powerful energies, vibrations and higher consciousness of spirit to flow freely in and through their whole being. When one creates this inner space within, ones higher self and all its virtues and gifts may fully inhabit and function in them.

Pranic Energy – Is the energy of life giving substance and contains electrical and magnetic particles.

Raising Consciousness – This involves changing the quality of ones consciousness and the pattern of ones experience to a higher level of manifestation.

Raising Frequency Levels - Anytime anyone reaches up to God Source and speaks from their heart through prayers, decrees or invocations, or through meditation, it immediately raises their vibrational frequency level to a higher octave and by doing so, it also increases the frequency level and octave of the planet.

Rebirth – Rebirth is the passing from an old condition into a new state.

Resurrection Dispensation – In this century, the Lords of Karma accorded humanity a new dispensation, whereby they can make their ascension with only 51 percent of their personal karma balanced and their life's mission and purpose fulfilled. It is the beginning of restoring humanity on their journey back to Divine life, love and purpose. The Violet Flame is to be used for this purpose in order to purify the four lower bodies. The Violet Flame is an aspect of the Holy Spirit that actually transmutes negative karma back to its original pristine essence of light. It still requires great diligence within each individual to do this work and emerge victorious.

This is no longer being offered the must exceed at 100% Karma erased.

Reincarnational Cycle – From the view of the soul, each incarnation on Earth is a new chance to get closer to its return

237

back to the divine state of origin. The soul always incarnates voluntarily.

Rod of Asclepius – The staff of Asclepius, the true symbol of medicine - denotes a healer.

Root Chakra – The root chakra is the first chakra which is located at the base of the spine. It is the energy centre that establishes the deepest connections with one's physical body, one's environment and with the Earth. It is the most instinctual chakra and is concerned primarily with survival.

Spirit - The spirit is the non-physical essence of the being that one knows as oneself. It is the self without a physical body that is free from time and space. This spirit is merely one facet of the multidimensional person that one really is.

Soul – One's Soul helps them to become the higher self they aspire to be. One's Soul is the force one reaches to when one is seeking any guidance or aid related to their present growth and evolution.

THE GREAT INVOCATION - (from the books of A.A. Bailey) The Great Invocation was given to humanity as a potent technique of invoking the energies which would transform the world. It belongs to all humanity and all humanity is urged to use it daily and encourage others to do so, on behalf of humanity.

The Great Work – To assist humanity in the attainment of the perfection of self so that they can transcend the lower dimensions of the human experience into a higher consciousness and reality thereby gaining ascension and ultimately, resurrection.

Transduce – A transducer is a device which converts one form of energy into another and is the process of stepping down the energy of creation from Source into form. The human body has a tremendous ability to transduce higher energies from the cosmos to be stepped down in frequency to flow through them into the Earth in order to facilitate transformation upon the Earth in a way that safely facilitates this process.

White Light - White Light contains all the frequencies of the visible range of the color spectrum and appears white to the human eye. It is of the highest frequency and is often called upon by healers for protection from negative energies and for healing purposes.

CPSIA information can be obtained
at www.ICGtesting.com
Printed in the USA
LVOW13s1914140518
577114LV00039B/1622/P

9 780994 889409